HEARING ON EDUCATION STANDARDS

WEDNESDAY, MARCH 22, 1995

HOUSE OF REPRESENTATIVES,
SUBCOMMITTEE ON OVERSIGHT AND INVESTIGATIONS,
COMMITTEE ON ECONOMIC AND
EDUCATIONAL OPPORTUNITIES,
Washington, DC.

The subcommittee met, pursuant to call, at 10 a.m., Room 2175, Rayburn House Office Building, Hon. Pete Hoekstra, Chairman, presiding.

Members present: Representatives Hoekstra, Barrett, Ballenger, Cunningham, McKeon, Castle, Weldon, Sawyer, Martinez, Roemer, and Green.

Staff present: John Barth, Professional Staff Member; Deanna Waldron, Staff Assistant; Dr. June L. Harris, Education Coordinator, and Sara Davis, Legislative Associate.

Chairman HOEKSTRA. Good morning. The Oversight Committee will now come to order. I just want to reiterate the principles of this subcommittee, as we continue our work and our investigation over the next 21 months.

We have said that we will continue to focus on what the appropriate Federal mission is in the labor and education areas. We want to ensure that the work in the Federal agencies is effective and efficient. We also want to ensure that the agencies work consistently to follow the objectives of our congressional intent. Over these next two years, one of the things that we want to do is to ensure that we have established a framework for policy initiatives that will create an environment for life-long learning and effective workplace policy, and that we will provide for a Federal Government role only where absolutely necessary.

The hearings that we have scheduled today, where we are going to take a look at gathering information about what the appropriate Federal role is in establishing national education guidelines, fits in very clearly with these overall objectives of the subcommittee, identifying exactly what the appropriate Federal mission is and establishing a framework for policy initiatives to encourage life-long learning.

I look forward to the hearing today. As is the custom of the Economic and Educational Opportunities Committee, any member is free to submit a written opening statement as part of the record. I'd like to turn it over to the Ranking Member, Mr. Sawyer, before we go to our first witness.

Mr. SAWYER. Thank you, Mr. Chairman. I do have an opening statement that I will submit for the record, but if I could just take a moment to summarize, let me begin by thanking you for rescheduling this hearing. I think that the kind of work that is done at these kinds of hearings really does establish that important framework for the work that we do in other subcommittees and in this committee as a whole.

I don't think there is a more important issue than the education standards, at least in terms of education issues that will come before this committee, because they do represent exactly that kind of framework and, to the degree that we can get them right, we have an obligation to do so.

I think it's important to remember that those standards began with the Education Summit convened by the President and the governors in Charlottesville, in 1989, and the goal there was to move off of "hot-button" rhetoric and into more solid ground where neutral analyses of deficiencies and areas of excellence could be fairly measured.

It was there that the six goals were agreed to, and it is there that this debate began. Two of those goals refer to student achievement. They are Goal 3, which covers a broad range of subjects, and Goal 4, which has a very compelling expectation that the United States be first in the world in mathematics and science by the end of this century.

The kind of work that has taken place since then in the establishment of the National Goals Panel, and the work to monitor progress and to get broad national acceptance of those goals has been enormously important. The work that involved both Governors Carroll Campbell and Roy Roemer, to recognize that the absence of explicit national standards keyed to world class levels of performance severely hampers our ability to monitor the Nation's progress towards those goals.

And so that National Council, which was chaired by that bipartisan pair of governors, recommended the development of school content, student performance standards, and system performance standards.

That recommendation went forward and yielded the criteria for voluntary national standards and voluntary State standards that would be submitted by the States. None of this is required, it's all strictly voluntary.

That is how we arrived at this point today, and now I know we're getting to the difficult part.

Perhaps the best analysis was in the suggestion that the complexity of the challenge guarantees that doing it right will be hard; "doing it wrong will be easy." I'm confident that this hearing will strengthen our effort to do it right. And, again, let me thank you for your effort to move that process forward.

[The prepared statement of Mr. Sawyer follows:]

STATEMENT OF HON. THOMAS C. SAWYER, A REPRESENTATIVE IN CONGRESS FROM THE STATE OF OHIO

Mr. Chairman: I want to thank you for rescheduling this hearing today because the issue of educational standards is, in my view, the most important education issue before this committee.

Let's review the bidding.

The development of voluntary national standards began with the Education Summit convened by Present Bush and the Nation's governors in Charlottesville, Virginia in 1989. In a very real sense, this Summit was a bipartisan effort to move

HEARING ON EDUCATION STANDARDS

HEARING

BEFORE THE

SUBCOMMITTEE ON OVERSIGHT AND INVESTIGATIONS

OF THE

COMMITTEE ON ECONOMIC AND EDUCATIONAL OPPORTUNITIES HOUSE OF REPRESENTATIVES

ONE HUNDRED FOURTH CONGRESS

FIRST SESSION

HEARING HELD IN WASHINGTON, DC, MARCH 22, 1995

Serial No. 104–17

Printed for the use of the Committee on Economic and Educational Opportunities

U.S. GOVERNMENT PRINTING OFFICE

92–107 CC WASHINGTON : 1995

For sale by the U.S. Government Printing Office
Superintendent of Documents, Congressional Sales Office, Washington, DC 20402
ISBN 0-16-047412-4

COMMITTEE ON ECONOMIC AND EDUCATIONAL OPPORTUNITIES

WILLIAM F. GOODLING, Pennsylvania, *Chairman*

THOMAS E. PETRI, Wisconsin
MARGE ROUKEMA, New Jersey
STEVE GUNDERSON, Wisconsin
HARRIS W. FAWELL, Illinois
CASS BALLENGER, North Carolina
BILL BARRETT, Nebraska
RANDY "DUKE" CUNNINGHAM, California
PETER HOEKSTRA, Michigan
HOWARD P. "BUCK" McKEON, California
MICHAEL N. CASTLE, Delaware
JAN MEYERS, Kansas
SAM JOHNSON, Texas
JAMES M. TALENT, Missouri
JAMES C. GREENWOOD, Pennsylvania
TIM HUTCHINSON, Arkansas
JOSEPH K. KNOLLENBERG, Michigan
FRANK D. RIGGS, California
LINDSEY O. GRAHAM, South Carolina
DAVE WELDON, Florida
DAVID FUNDERBURK, North Carolina
MARK SOUDER, Indiana
DAVID McINTOSH, Indiana
CHARLIE NORWOOD, Georgia

WILLIAM L. CLAY, Missouri
GEORGE MILLER, California
DALE E. KILDEE, Michigan
PAT WILLIAMS, Montana
MATTHEW G. MARTINEZ, California
MAJOR R. OWENS, New York
THOMAS C. SAWYER, Ohio
DONALD M. PAYNE, New Jersey
PATSY T. MINK, Hawaii
ROBERT E. ANDREWS, New Jersey
JACK REED, Rhode Island
TIM ROEMER, Indiana
ELIOT L. ENGEL, New York
XAVIER BECERRA, California
ROBERT C. SCOTT, Virginia
GENE GREEN, Texas
LYNN C. WOOLSEY, California
CARLOS A. ROMERO-BARCELÓ, Puerto Rico
MEL REYNOLDS, Illinois

JAY EAGEN, *Staff Director*
GAIL E. WEISS, *Minority Staff Director*

SUBCOMMITTEE ON OVERSIGHT AND INVESTIGATIONS

PETER HOEKSTRA, Michigan, *Chairman*

BILL BARRETT, Nebraska
CASS BALLENGER, North Carolina
RANDY "DUKE" CUNNINGHAM, California
HOWARD P. "BUCK" McKEON, California
MICHAEL N. CASTLE, Delaware
DAVID WELDON, Florida
WILLIAM F. GOODLING, Pennsylvania
HARRIS W. FAWELL, Illinois

THOMAS C. SAWYER, Ohio
MATTHEW G. MARTINEZ, California
JACK REED, Rhode Island
TIM ROEMER, Indiana
ROBERT C. "BOBBY" SCOTT, Virginia
GENE GREEN, Texas
MEL REYNOLDS, Illinois

CONTENTS

the debate over education reform from the ether of hot-button rhetoric onto neutral ground where deficiencies and areas of excellence could be fairly measured.

At the Summit, the participants agreed to establish six educational goals. These goals were formally adopted by the Governors and President Bush in 1990.

It is *here* that the real issue of the debate lies.

Two of those goals refer to student achievement. Goal 3 states that "by the year 2000, all students will leave grades 4, 8 and 12 *having demonstrated competency over challenging subject matter,* including English, mathematics, science, foreign languages, civics and government, economics, arts, history and geography, and every school in America will insure that all students learn to use their minds well, so that they may be prepared for responsible citizenship, further learning, and productive employment in our modern economy."

Goal 4 states that "... by the year 2000, United States students will be first in the world in *mathematics and science.*"

After the goals were established, President Bush and the governors created the National Education Goals Panel to encourage broad acceptance of these national goals and to *monitor progress on the goals.*

As the Goals Panel convened, the members needed more explicit criteria to monitor progress in student achievement and inform the Nation about the progress American students were making [or not making] on competency in challenging subject matter and their level of math and science achievement. What did competence in math mean—particularly in terms of world class competition?

The *National Council on Education Standards and Testing*, NCEST, was established to advise the Congress, the administration and the Goals Panel on how to develop standards and related assessments. This bipartisan panel issued their report six months later. The Co-chairs [Carroll Campbell and Roy Romer] wrote:

> "... the absence of explicit national standards keyed to world class levels of performance severely hampers our ability to monitor the Nation's progress towards the National Education Goals."

The National Council recommended the development of for-school-content and student performance standards, and system performance standards. The report proposed that the Goals Panel, together with a new *National Education Standards and Assessments Council* would certify content and student performance standards.

These recommendations were substantially incorporated within Goals 2000. Title II in 1994. Under Title II, the National Education Standards and Improvement Council [NESIC] works together with the National Education Goals Panel to establish criteria for certification and to review, analyze and certify **voluntary** national standards submitted by professional organizations, and State standards voluntarily submitted by the States. *None* of this is required, submission of standards for certification is *strictly voluntary.*

Mr. Chairman, that is how we arrived at this point. The only problem, as I see it, is that now we are getting to the difficult part. I recently saw a good description of the status of standards setting: "that the complexity of the challenge guarantees that doing it right will be hard; doing it wrong will be easy."

I am confident that this hearing will strengthen our resolve not to take the path of least resistance.

I look forward to hearing from our distinguished witnesses.

Chairman HOEKSTRA. Thank you. The process this morning is that we will have two panels. The first panel will be a distinguished colleague from the other body. We'd like to invite Senator Jeff Bingaman. Welcome, thank you for being with us this morning.

Senator Bingaman is a member of the National Education Goals Panel. Thank you for being here, and we are looking forward to your testimony.

STATEMENT OF HON. JEFF BINGAMAN, A SENATOR IN CONGRESS FROM THE STATE OF NEW MEXICO

Senator BINGAMAN. Thank you very much, Mr. Chairman. It's a pleasure to be here. I do have the honor to serve on the National Education with the Chairman of the full committee, Congressman Goodling, and I believe that the work of that Education Goals Panel is very important.

Let me just at the opening, before going into what I planned to say, indicate to everybody, in case there is any confusion about it, the National Education Goals Panel is an organization dominated by State elected officials.

There are 18 members of the National Education Goals Panel, 12 of them are State elected officials—eight governors and four representatives from State legislatures—so it is not a Federal Government entity, as such.

It is somewhat unique, when you think about national panels, at least in my experience. I don't know of another national panel that we have set up intentionally to give the primary authority to the States, but the National Education Goals Panel is organized that way—I think appropriately organized that way—because of the recognition that States and local government have the primary responsibility, historically in our country, for education policy. The Federal Government is a participant, and the Secretary of Education is on that panel, as he should be, but the majority of the members are, in fact, State elected officials.

As Congressman Sawyer indicated, the goals that were established by President Bush and the governors who met in Charlottesville, in 1989, contained Goal 3, which spoke about proficiency in core academic subjects, and how that was to be a major goal of this country between now and the year 2000.

Obviously, in order to monitor the progress toward that goal, we needed to have some definition of what we mean by proficiency. And the conclusion was that if we were going to seriously pursue reform, it was not going to be adequate to continue as we have all the time that I've been both a student and a parent in the educational system—continue to implore our schools to do better, but not give them any indication of what proficiency consists of.

The thought was that we need some uniformity of expectation so that we can compare performances from one school to another school, compare performances from one State to another State.

Parents and teachers and school administrators and legislators in my home State of New Mexico need to know whether the students that are coming out of our school system are going to be comparably prepared to those students who are graduating in Colorado, or Arizona, or Texas.

And there's also a national interest. I was reviewing an Op-Ed piece by Checker Finn, who is well recognized for his expertise in this area—a former Assistant Secretary of Education. He wrote a piece shortly before the meeting of the Charlottesville Summit, where he made the point very convincingly, I thought, in talking about why we need a national norm, not just State norms. He said this is a Nation that is at risk, not just Oklahoma or Pennsylvania. It's the whole country that is competing with Korea, Germany, and Japan.

And I do think that there is a need for some ability to compare our students to each other across State lines, and also internationally, and determine whether we are, in fact, expecting of them what students are expected to do in other countries.

We already do have national standards, and I think anybody who will look at it has to acknowledge that there are national standards in place today. We have one set of standards for a very few of our students, which I would say are the advanced placement course standards.

If you take an advanced placement course anywhere in this country, in American History, you have a standard that you are held to which is agreed upon, which is pretty high, and which our post-secondary schools, our universities, give some serious respect to.

Most of our students, though, are not held to those standards. Most of our students are held to the standards that the textbook writers set.

There is a very interesting study, which I recommend to the committee, that was done at Cornell University just about a year and a half ago. In 1993, at the end of 1993, it was published by Donald Hayes and Loreen Wolfer. The study essentially goes through and analyzes textbooks that have been used in our elementary and secondary schools since the second World War. It concludes that we have "dumbed-down" the textbooks in this country since the second World War, and that we have essentially allowed the textbook writers to determine what level of performance we were going to teach to, what level of performance we were going to hold our students to, and, all too often, that has resulted in diminished expectations and diminished performance.

The point that is obvious that we are shortchanging our students as the world is becoming more challenging; as the competition that they are facing is becoming more challenging, we are expecting less of them.

The materials we provide to them in the way of textbooks, the instruction we provide to them through our teachers, is preparing them less well for the effort.

I know a major issue that is being debated is whether or not there ought to be a national mechanism to essentially have some responsibility for judging standards that are determined State-by-State. I feel very strongly there should be. I think that, otherwise, you have a balkanization of the system.

I don't think it should be a Federal group. I think it should be the National Education Goals Panel. My own belief is that that organization is constituted in a way that the States control it—that's the way it ought to be constituted. There needs to be a central place where States can take their proposed standards, if they want to—it will be on a voluntary basis—and say, how do my standards compare with Colorado, or how do my standards compare with world class standards? If we, in fact, teach to these standards, will our students be able to compete for jobs and demonstrate the proficiency they need to?

I believe we need to bring a national consensus to bear on these standards. If we don't have a source for authoritative comment, the entire effort will be balkanized.

We should have a great many people commenting anytime a proposed set of standards is issued. I think that's a very healthy process. That's the way our system ought to work. But there ought to be some group, nominated by the States, that say, "Yes, these standards meet the criteria that we think is appropriate."

States may improve. Many States are working very hard to improve. But I believe that they will be able to improve only marginally, and textbook companies will continue to determine what the standards for the country are, as a whole, unless we go forward with the standards-setting process at the national level.

The American public will continue to lack the information it needs to evaluate American education properly, and I think our local schools will suffer unless we go forward and go ahead and implement standards.

That's all I have to say, Mr. Chairman. I'm glad to respond to any questions anybody has, otherwise, I'll defer to the very distinguished group of experts that you've assembled for your hearing today.

Chairman HOEKSTRA. Are there any Members on the panel that would have a question? Mr. Ballenger?

Mr. BALLENGER. Senator, I was just curious, when you say the standards have been, or the teaching has been "dumbed-down," and the goals and standards on the committee on which you sit, are the standards going to be set for the best students, or the average students?

In your study there, are you actually aiming to set a goal that's reachable by only a few?

Senator BINGAMAN. No. As I—and I'm sure each of the other panelists you will hear from today will have their own response to that question—but my own view is that we should set standards which are achievable by the vast majority of our students.

Now, some are going to have to work harder to achieve those standards than others, but I think that we're trying to focus on outcomes, and we're trying to say if a person is going to be proficient in fourth-grade mathematics, they ought to be able to do the following things, and that should not be something that just a few of the students can accomplish. Each of the students who graduate from the fourth grade should try to achieve that level of proficiency.

Now, obviously, there are a lot of differences in individual capacity, but I think the standards we are trying to set are high standards, but they are standards that apply to the average student in our country.

Chairman HOEKSTRA. I'm going to be just a little informal with the questioning because I believe the Senator has another commitment.

Senator BINGAMAN. That's fine, but I do have time, if there are any other questions.

Chairman HOEKSTRA. I would like to yield to Mr. Sawyer.

Mr. SAWYER. Thank you, Mr. Chairman. I just wanted to thank the Senator for being here. Your experience and your thoughtful comments are useful, as we guide our process here. Grateful for your being here. I understand Mr. Roemer has a question.

Chairman HOEKSTRA. Mr. Roemer.

Mr. ROEMER. Senator, I would like to thank you for joining us on the House side this morning, too. And I just have one brief question.

We have our material here today with a lot of these standards. Whether you are for them or against them, who would you recommend review the quality of these standards?

Senator BINGAMAN. Well, I believe that the National Education Goals Panel is the one entity in the country that is properly organized and constituted to have that ultimate responsibility. It's a group of politicians, but they are politicians who are accountable at the State level primarily, a few at the national level, but I do believe that that's the right group.

Now, clearly, they need expert advice, and they would have to set up an advisory group, or perhaps several advisory groups, to advise them on individual standards that are presented, before they would pass judgment. But I think they could go through a process of getting comments, soliciting comments from a variety of groups and individuals, and then getting their own advice from experts who they respect, and come up with something which would have the support of the eight governors on that panel, would have the support of the four legislators on that panel, would have the support of the two House Members on the panel—your Chairman included—and the two Senate Members, and the Secretary of Education as well. So, I think that's the best way to proceed.

Mr. ROEMER. What if that turned into something that was cumbersome and difficult to do, would you support local standards as an alternative?

Senator BINGAMAN. Well, I think all of the standards are going to be local. I mean, the whole way this thing is designed, States or local school districts would develop their standards, and then would submit them for comment or review, if they chose to do that. If they chose not to, then obviously there would be no review of them.

But Governor Romer, who has been a real stalwart and champion of this whole effort for many years—the Governor of Colorado—he makes a very good point. He says, we have prepared some standards in Colorado. We want to know where we can take those to get someone to tell us, are these world class standards? How do they compare with the other States? Is there somebody around the country who is doing better than we are proposing to do? That's what he wants out of the process, and that's what I think a national organization should be able to do—something like the National Education Goals Panel—in the standards area.

Mr. ROEMER. So you see no conflict between the Goals 2000 Advisory Committee working with Governor Roemer's standards and his committee in order to work out both the policy by which these are locally devised standards, but which, if the Governor feels that he is falling behind in an area or two, he can get advice, although not mandates, from this Goals 2000 group?

Senator BINGAMAN. No, I understand that's the way the process is supposed to work. It is to encourage each State to go through a standards-setting process. It is to encourage local school districts to go through standards-setting processes within those States. And then it is to have some mechanism for giving feedback and saying, these are not up-to-par. These standards do not meet the standard that other States are aspiring to. And you need to know that. I mean, that's the kind of feedback that some governors have indicated they would like.

And as I say, it would be purely on a voluntary basis. I don't see this group as going around and offering advice that hasn't been requested.

Mr. ROEMER. Thank you, Senator.

Chairman HOEKSTRA. Mr. Castle.

Mr. CASTLE. Senator, I actually was the governor in 1989, and went to Charlottesville and set the goals. To me, it was a wonderful process. The President was very involved in it, and the goals were relatively simplistic.

Now I look at these books on standards and, all of a sudden, it's a proliferation of information, and I worry a little bit about it. Can any of us grasp—particularly you all, who are really carrying this out—can we really grasp what these standards are, or are they getting to the point that it's just so inclusive that it includes anything anybody would say is a standard. I just have a little trouble with that.

Senator BINGAMAN. No, I think that's a very valid concern. And one of the big jobs of a central review organization would be to say, this is too much. I mean, you cannot—a student is going to have to take quite a few subjects in their fourth grade, or in their eighth grade, or in their tenth grade class. You cannot expect them to become a Ph.D. in American History, or in mathematics, or whatever.

So, I think that integrating them and coming up with some reasonable standard for what we expect students to do is an important part of it because I agree with you, some of the standards are way too extensive at this point—some of the proposed standards. I should point out that none of the proposed standards that you have copies of, have been approved by anybody.

Mr. CASTLE. Oh, is that right? I'm glad to know that.

Senator BINGAMAN. Yes. The National Education Goals Panel has not taken upon itself a review of any of these. There are all these things floating around and, quite frankly, I'm afraid that if we don't have a mechanism for review, you're going to have a proliferation. You're going to have a stack three times as high as the one you've got there, of different competing standards, which the average school administrator or teacher is going to just think, "This is crazy. I can't make sense out of this."

So, I think that you're right, there's too much coming out.

Mr. CASTLE. Let me just—and I don't know this, so I need to follow up on it—and I think I agree with you, the National Education Goals Panel is the place to do this. You have said that the States should be able to review their standards in comparison with other States, and I don't have a problem with any of that.

But let me know—I don't know if you said this or not, but it's implicit in what you are saying—are you suggesting that we have testing and results as another end-game of all of this setting of standards?

Senator BINGAMAN. Well, I think that any of the States that set standards, are going to want to have some way of assessing whether their students achieve those standards.

Mr. CASTLE. And should we have State-by-State comparisons, and district-by-district comparisons?

Senator BINGAMAN. Well, I think the way the thing is envisioned, as I understand it now, there is not to be a national test. There undoubtedly would grow up some tests which would be essentially shared by certain clusters of States, that determine that, yes, our standards are similar to Colorado's, we want to use that as a benchmark, and we would use their assessment tools or some variation of that, which would give us an ability to use them as a benchmark.

Mr. CASTLE. Well, I guess I go a little bit beyond that. I almost believe in the testing—I was on the National Assessment Governing Board for a while, and we did some State-by-State comparisons in testing and, frankly—Pat Forgione is here and is going to testify—but before he came to Delaware, I was a little concerned that Delaware was not doing as well as I thought we were, and I'll tell you, it motivated me. I mean, we pumped more money into education. We went out and sought the best educator we could find, to come into the State. I mean, we did everything we could. And I just think some of that—people shy from that—but I think some of it works as well. I just don't know how that ties into what the National Education Goals Panel is doing in standards-setting. That's the reason I raised the question.

Senator BINGAMAN. Well, it's down the road a little bit, in the list of tasks that they are really focused on at this point, but I think clearly there has got to be—each State that sets standards is going to have to have a mechanism for assessing how they are doing and, as you point out, being able to make comparisons with other States.

Mr. CASTLE. Thank you, Senator. Thank you, Mr. Chairman.

Chairman HOEKSTRA. Mr. Green.

Mr. GREEN. Thank you, Mr. Chairman. I'll be very brief, Senator. Your testimony concerning the dumbing-down of our textbooks for a number of years—and I know, having—and, again, I preface almost everything I say because I was trained for 20 years in the Texas Legislature, and we didn't want us adopting textbooks by the legislature, but we had a system created. And, typically, when you have in large States—Texas, California, New York—large book purchasers, they are the ones that really can set the standards for the Nation. And we don't want to do it here in Washington, but—and I know what's happening, literally, in Austin, Texas, as we sit here today, and may be happening in Sacramento and Albany, too—that by having these standards, we can overall influence what these larger States are doing, and have the positive impact on those textbooks that you want to see improve.

And I was glad to see Governor Castle talk about that because it's not—these are national standards, and they are voluntary, as you said, but the real battle is often in the State capitals and the local school board meetings because that's where the standards are really going to be enforced, and some of those comparisons, some of the tests—we don't need a national test because we have tests being required now by a great many States, and the comparisons are available because they use national standardized tests and we can compare State-to-State.

I know, in Texas, we compare district-to-district, and school-to-school within our districts. So, I was glad to hear the concern because, over a period of years, we have to continue the momentum.

Again, I was in the legislature when Nation At Risk was released, and part of that group of States that tried to respond, in the mid 1980s, to it, like Delaware and Tennessee, and we see now some moderating, I guess, some of that emphasis from the mid 1980s, and we need to continue that intensity not only in the Capitol here, but particularly in the State capitals because it's not something where you can say, well, we did that in 1985 or 1986, and it's over. We have to continue those efforts, and I think the national goals gives those States, like you said, Colorado, something that they can compare to and shoot for. Thank you, Mr. Chairman.

Chairman HOEKSTRA. Mr. Barrett.

Mr. BARRETT. I, too, thank you, Senator, for sharing your thoughts on education standards with us today. A thought occurred to me that the panel or the council that you referred to in reviewing and certifying standards, could this not be viewed in the eyes of some, as a National School Board? Is that a distinct possibility? And, if so, what should this Congress be doing to address it, if anything?

Senator BINGAMAN. Well, I don't really think there's much comparison between what the National Education Goals Panel is trying to take on, and a school board. It has no authority to do anything. It's a group that responds—in the standard area—responds to requests from States, that voluntarily bring things to it and say, "please tell me where we stand on that."

I think the consensus—and other Members here can speak about it—but I think the consensus on the National Education Goals Panel is that they would not want to even certify standards. They would want to give feedback. They would want to essentially point out deficiencies where they exist, or where they believe they exist, in a State's standards, but they would not certify, in any kind of formalistic sense.

Let me just say that there is great sensitivity—as you can imagine, with eight governors and four State legislators—there is great sensitivity on the National Education Goals Panel, to the Federal Government or the national government not being too intrusive in what the States do. This is not a problem. I mean, we are not—the National Education Goals Panel is not about to run roughshod over the States because you've got 12 States represented right there.

But I think that it's very unlikely that anyone could persuasively argue that the National Education Goals Panel is becoming a national school board.

Mr. BARRETT. Thank you, I appreciate that answer.

Chairman HOEKSTRA. Mr. Weldon.

Mr. WELDON. Thank you, Mr. Chairman, and I thank the Senator for coming and testifying.

I believe most Americans can probably agree on national standards for math, perhaps for reading and writing and, indeed, I think those are probably the most important standards because those are the most important areas. Other than building character and virtue in our children—those are the most important areas that relate to employability and the possibility of having a successful career, and that's really the real standards-setter in our culture—whether our children are able to go out into the marketplace and be successful.

But when it comes to the areas of history and English and civics, I think there is a tremendous potential for a fair amount of contention on those issues because there are some individuals who would consider some areas more worth study in those realms, than others.

And as I understand it, there's already some controversy centering around the history standards that are being proposed. Some critics have approached me saying that more time and attention is devoted to the creation of the Sierra Club and the National Organization for Women, than there is to the creation of our Declaration of Independence and our Constitution.

Now, I don't know necessarily if those criticisms are accurate, and I need to study that, but, clearly, I see a major problem in this realm. Please share any comments you have for me regarding how you are wrestling with those issues and how they can be resolved.

Senator BINGAMAN. Well, I'll just give you my personal view on it. I think you are right, the study of math and science may not be as value-laden as the other areas you're talking about and, accordingly, not as subject to controversy.

I do think that it's possible to have national standards in the other areas, though, as long as they are carefully done and done in a balanced way. I think there are proposed civics standards which have been developed as part of the standards-setting process, which I believe have been well received on all sides.

Now, there is no area of our national life that is more value-laden than civics, and they evidently have done a good job in coming up with some guidelines there that people are willing to agree to.

In the history area, you are right, there is a lot of controversy about the proposed standards that were developed in that area, and I think that's the reason why you need something like the National Education Goals Panel, and you need to give them a chance to circulate any kind of proposed standard for comment, and then to respond on that, and take a position. I think that helps to deal with the very concern that you've got, and I think it's a valid concern.

We had a vote in the Senate, with an overwhelming vote indicating we did not think the proposed history standards, as they came out, should be adopted by the Goals Panel.

I urged Senator Gorton, who was the sponsor of that amendment, to not have us in the Congress directing the Goals Panel on what to do about this or any other standard. It seemed to me they should be given the authority that we intended that they have, to review standards and reach their own conclusion. I'm sure they would reach the right conclusion.

Chairman HOEKSTRA. Mr. Cunningham. Excuse the oversight, Mr. Cunningham. The Oversight Chairman has a little work to do yet in oversight of the committee.

Mr. CUNNINGHAM. Listen, I'm getting used to it—not just in this committee—but for some reason, I must be a tiny guy.

Senator, I'm glad to hear what you talked about in the standards because, in this committee, it's a very bipartisan issue—Dale Kildee, who is a history major, on the issue; Bill Goodling, who sits on the Panel——

Senator BINGAMAN. Dale Kildee sits on the Panel, too. I should have said that.

Mr. CUNNINGHAM. [continuing] and myself, met with the National Center for History in Schools, and talked about the history standards.

I guess my question, though, is, when you have a Goals Panel—when you meet in Charlottesville—would you support a better review of those because of what's happened. When we interviewed the doctor that wrote the civics standards, he was very flexible but, yet, when we met with the individual from the university that wrote the history standards, he was left of Karl Marx, and tried to justify those history standards.

And many of us feel that we want to put an emphasis on early American history instead of Madonna, instead of McCarthyism—although they should be included in some way—but, evidently, it has gone so far that we could have a crisis. And I really feel that if we hadn't taken over the majority, they would have been whisked right through.

And there's got to be some way in which your group can sit down and make those determinations before they get so far because they were already printed, and you know that costs a lot of dollars itself.

Senator BINGAMAN. They were printed as a result of a contract, which was let under the Bush Administration, to have them developed. And it was never intended that the standards would be approved or adopted or become the de facto standards, without some review and determination as to whether they were proper or not.

Mr. CUNNINGHAM. Because what happens is, you have a printing like this, and you know the commercial world, as soon as you get something like this, all the textbooks are starting to be printed with this kind of material in there. I think when we're going to establish these goals, and I totally laud what you're trying to do, but I believe, personally, that we need just a little bit more oversight before it gets to this stage because, once those commercial units and the textbooks start getting printed, that becomes the standard.

Senator BINGAMAN. I agree, and I think you make the case better than I have, for having a group like the National Education Goals Panel that has to sign off on something before they become a national standard, a national de facto standard, because you're right, if there's not something else that intervenes, then everybody will assume, well, these things are printed, they must be—they say national on them, maybe this is the real thing. So, you have to have a system for review, which has not taken place yet.

Mr. CUNNINGHAM. Thank you, Senator. And Karl Marx did yield, Mr. Kildee made sure that he did. Thank you.

Senator BINGAMAN. Karl Marx did what now?

Mr. CUNNINGHAM. The guy that wrote the history standard, he did yield.

Senator BINGAMAN. Oh, I see, the guy who wrote the standard.

Mr. CUNNINGHAM. Dale Kildee and Chairman Goodling took care of that real quick.

Senator BINGAMAN. All right. Thank you. Thank you very much, Mr. Chairman.

Chairman HOEKSTRA. Thank you.

I'd like to invite the second panel to please come forward. I'd like to welcome the panel to the committee hearing. I'd like to yield to my colleague from Delaware for an introduction.

I'd like to invite the second panel to please come forward. I'd like to welcome the panel to the committee hearing. I'd like to yield to my colleague from Delaware for an introduction.

Mr. CASTLE. Thank you very much, Mr. Chairman. I've already mentioned Dr. Forgione. I know some of the other members as well, but I've worked with Pat Forgione. We were fortunate to be able to hire him after he had been the Executive Director—while he was the Executive Director, I should say—of the National Education Goals Panel, so he has a lot of knowledge about the standards we are talking about. He has also been the Superintendent of Public Instruction in the State of Delaware, for several years now, and has led an effort there called New Directions, which is aimed at carrying out at the State level some of the things we're talking about here on the national level. So, Pat, we're delighted to have you here, and look forward to your testimony, as well as to the others.

Chairman HOEKSTRA. Thank you. The rest of the members of the panel include Lynne Cheney, who is currently with the American Enterprise Institute, and also former Chair of the National Endowment for the Humanities. We also have Albert Shanker, who is President of the American Federation of Teachers. We also have with us Dr. Ravitch, who is associated with the New York University and recently published a book entitled National Standards in America: A Citizen's Guide, which may be the first thing we should read. We've all been holding up different things, but these, I guess, are the compilation today of the first shot at national standards, and maybe we ought to read your book before we read any of these because your book may actually be in language that we can understand.

And then representing the business community, we have Mr. James Burge, Corporate Vice President of Motorola. Welcome, and we will begin with you, Dr. Forgione.

STATEMENT OF DR. PASCAL D. FORGIONE, SUPERINTENDENT OF PUBLIC INSTRUCTION, STATE OF DELAWARE

Dr. FORGIONE. Good morning, Representative Hoekstra, Members of the subcommittee, ladies and gentlemen. I'm very pleased to be participating this morning in this very timely and important hearing on educational standards.

I'm sure I was invited to participate so that I could bring a concrete and ground-level view to what's happening in States and districts as we confront this important work of building academic standards and expectations for our public schools, and ensuring that we achieve enhanced performance by our students, our Nation's most precious resource.

I have submitted my written testimony, which focuses on Delaware's agenda called New Direction for Education in Delaware. We're in our third year of a five-year plan.

I think the committee would be interested to know that partnership is taken serious in Delaware, and I have 19 school districts—it's a blessing, only 19—but each school district has voted each of three years, to commit $5 per student out of their own budget—we have 100,000 children, so the math isn't too difficult—they are donating a half a million dollars, and the business community is think owning something means you have to contribute and, by contributing, you take a stake in it.

My testimony outlines a practical common sense strategy that my State has taken to launch the preparation of our young children for college, for the world of work, and for the 21st century, and it's only five years away.

My paper provides actual experiences that my State has encountered in building broad and deep agreement on a statewide level. As Representative Castle knows, from Delmar to Brandywine, it's a long State. How do you build deep agreement across 6,800 classrooms, across parents and the business community? That's the challenge ahead of us, to make these standards documents. We've printed them in newspaper format because the middle of it you send back to us, and we want to let you know they're drafts—because we've got to let America and Delaware own these because that's the key to standards—agreement, consensus—and we're taking six months to go through this before it becomes real, so that Delaware will have a solid foundation on standards.

But we also need to build assessments. How do you measure this? How do we know we're building progress? And the third piece, besides standards and assessment, we've got to invest in the capacity of our system to deliver to these high-challenging levels. It's not going to be easy, but we, in public education, really want to do that for our children.

These standards are different. In the old days, we were about inputs and processes, and now we're about academic results. And the development of academic standards is a foundational activity, and it goes back to the partnership that was just mentioned. At Charlottesville, where the States and governors came together and had a compact that we will, in fact, build on the foundation of the national goals in Goal 3, student achievement in civics, Goal 4, science and math.

I'd like to share with you—that's not in my testimony—some comments I have about the Educate America: Goals 2000, Title II, as part of my oral testimony, and I'll type this up and submit it later.

I'd like to make three key points up front, that I think are key to educational standards. The first point is, let's remember why we're all about this important work of enhancing standards. I'm wearing a button today, that I wear every day, that reminds me of what my responsibility is as a public education official—children first. Children first.

We need to continually remind ourselves of our raison d'étre. We need a Federal investment in our children's development, and we need that coordinated with our State and local efforts. Children first.

The second feature I think that I'd like to present to you is the strategy we've chosen to go forward on—the National Goals. They are at the heart of where we're going.

Wayne Gretzky was once asked what made him such a great hockey player. "Because", he said, "I go where the puck is going, not where it is." And that's what standards can do for us, for our children across this country, and we need to "go for the gold" for our children. And these are national, not Federal standards, but not where it is." And that's what standards can do for us, for our children across this country, and we need to "go for the gold" for our children. And these are national, not Federal standards, but they've got to be stretch standards that reach the goals and the standards. They've got to stretch us.

I believe the initial work that's underway has been bipartisan, consensual, and leadership-oriented, but I would ask the committee to reaffirm our shared commitment up to the national goals, and the necessary partnership of the Federal Government in supporting the momentum that's underway in some 33 States. We're going for it. We're on our way. Be our partner. Be "wind in our sails." So, children first, the national goals second.

And the third point I want to State is that it's absolutely appropriate and vital that we have a Federal role in supporting educational standards. The Federal role, I believe, is necessary and needs to be crafted with an emphasis on two dimensions—voluntary national standards, with multiple models and rich examples because, from that multiplicity, we in Delaware will select what's best for us. We need that, but we can't do it alone. It's so hard to do it alone.

We also want flexibility in the support of the direction we choose to go ahead. Give us flexibility. I would support the subcommittee's fine-tuning elements in Title II of Goals 2000. I would support your removing NESIC provision, the certification of standards, and the opportunity to learn standards. I don't believe they are essential because I believe they are dividing us, but I would add, I strongly endorse the other provisions of Title II.

And I wish the committee to know, as we develop these standards in Delaware, we had four commissions, cochaired by teachers, with 25 teachers on each. We can do it right in Delaware because we're small, and you can go home at night and be in your bed. Teachers had to lead this, with parents and business members, but I want you to know, there is not one instance I have where the national work to date has impeded upon our decision of what's good for Delaware.

We selected some, we rejected some. We, in fact, have examples of where we influence the nationals. So, I want you to know that, the national standards have not impaired us. We are about a reflective act, and we will do it right through Delaware, but we appreciate your oversight because you want the same thing we want for our children. Your investment is critical to us—the national compact to make this happen.

I'd like to give you two quick examples of recently how you need to work together. I have just received the national science standard. And I want you to know—it's only two hours from Dover to downtown Washington—we met with the National Research Council over a year ago, and we have arm-twisted with them because we told them they didn't have solutions, liquid solutions, in their science standard. They have adjusted. So, it was a receiving and a giving, but we were lucky to get in there and to duke it out with them because you've got to duke it out. You've got to own it and think it through.

So, I want to say, these science standards really reflect deliberation today, and now my commission and our National Science

Foundation Systemic Initiative Grant, they are reviewing them to find gaps and to tell us where we're going.

I'd like to urge you not to extend any cutoff of funds to the preparation and dissemination of materials, especially to such good, voluntary work, grassroots work, like the National Standards in Science. These standards and the math standards need to be moved forward so that States can build their own curriculum.

We build the curriculum. And in Delaware, the 19 districts will build the curriculum, not Dover. That's a local school act that we'll support. We've got to be clear about our roles and responsibilities. And in my paper, in Figure 4 on page 11, we tried to clarify what's the State's role and what's the local's role because that's not been always clear within our own States, and I'm sure each of you have stories about that.

The second example I wanted to give you of how important your investment is, in the area of science again, but it illustrates that you need an active and purposeful focused Federal role.

The Delaware science curriculum, we found out, is incoherent and of poor quality, and we want to be world class. But the cochair of this science commission is the head scientist at Dupont, the premier scientist in the whole world for Dupont. He was in Japan in the Fall of 1993. He picked up the Japanese science textbook, in Japanese, and brought it back. His company translated that into English for us, and our commission has been using that for a year and a half.

What does it mean? Why do they do it that way? Why do they have that order? What is the thinking? It took us a year and a half to understand it, to decide what was good for Delaware and what isn't. By that provision of having that work available, Delaware was fortunate that Dupont was willing to do that.

But our future should not be conditioned on such fortunate circumstances in this instance, that we got access to an English translation—that we haven't shared with anyone else, by the way—because there's parochialism in it.

The Federal investment in developing and disseminating voluntarily is an asset and a prerequisite to assisting States and districts in making the most of our current standards and development work.

Moreover, I see three areas that you certainly should have a Federal role in—development of content assessment outside the basics, in science, in speaking, in listening. We need your help in that.

Linking research so we can link State assessments to each other and to national. There's research that has to be done so we can use Delaware's assessment, but know how we compare.

And the third area is international benchmarks. We need your help in doing that because I can't go to Germany and Taiwan, I'm too small. No one listens when Delaware talks, but if a consortium of States could be funded, we could do that together.

So, in conclusion, I respectively request on behalf of my colleague States, that you please stay the course and not dismantle Goals 2000. Please fulfill our national goals partnership responsibility in concert with your colleague States as part of our shared commitment to effecting academic performance for all of our children.

The State of Delaware can't do it alone, and we don't want to do it alone. Without a focused Federal effort to ensure excellence and equity for all of America's children, we will not make the progress we could. Thank you.

[The prepared statement of Dr. Forgione follows:]

Pascal D. Forgione, Jr., Ph.D.
State Superintendent of Public Instruction
Department of Public Instruction

A State Perspective on Education Standards: A Delaware Experience

Thank you. I am pleased to be invited to participate this morning in this important and timely hearing on "Education Standards" by the U.S. House of Representatives' Subcommittee on Oversight and Investigations. I am sure that my participation is intended to offer a concrete and ground level view of the realities that states and local districts are confronting in the important and hard education improvement work to raise academic expectations for our public schools and to achieve enhanced academic performance by all our students, the nation's most precious resource.

I will center my commentary on the actual experiences that my state has encountered in our efforts to build deep and broad agreement statewide on more rigorous academic standards in the core diciplines of mathematics, science, English language arts and social studies (civics/economics/geography/history) and to design and implement new assessment or testing systems that will regularly monitor the progress of Delaware public schools and students in achieving our shared academic goals. Fortunately, Delaware's approach is reflective of and largely comparable to at least some three dozen other states nationally who are proceeding to implement standards-based education reform initiatives.

This standards-based education policy direction is a dramatic shift from the prior focus on education inputs and processes to an emphasis on academic results. Thus, the development of challenging academic standards is a foundational activity that is a prerequisite for our fulfilling the jointly agreed to commitment that the Governors and states endorsed in 1989 as part of the National Education Goals at the Charlottesville Education Summit, namely: student achievement and citizenship goal; and science and mathematics goals.

For the next few minutes I want to talk with you about Delaware's public schools and how we can make them better. I'll outline a practical, common sense strategy to prepare our young people for college, for work and for life in the 21st century -- which is only five years away.

The Value of An Education

Three current realities convince me that nothing less than basic change will assure our children's, and our society's future. One, unless you're a gifted athlete or entertainer, a good education is the only route to a successful and rewarding life. Two, the work place is changing fast and employees must know more and be able to do more than in the past. And, three, large numbers of kids are leaving school today -- before or after graduation -- without the skills they need to succeed in life.

The most tangible evidence of what a good education is worth today comes in earning power. A four-year college degree on average is worth 75 percent more over a working lifetime than a high school degree. That's a huge incentive.

Education has always been an economic winner, but its relative value is soaring. At the same time a larger portion of new jobs require higher skills. The result is a widening gap between those with marketable skills and those without them. Delaware kids need those skills to succeed.

Societal Benefits of An Educated Citizenry

A good education benefits not only our young people and their families. It's also important to us as citizens, for a well educated population attracts new business and improves the standard of living for us all. It also helps us get along together as a society and reduces the cost of government over the long run. Consider that seven of ten inmates in Delaware prisons lack a high school diploma and that some 60 percent of Delaware welfare mothers did not finish high school.

So it's in our self interest -- whether or not we have children in school -- to see that Delawareans are well educated. In fact, a recent Delaware pool found that 98 percent of Delawareans consider education "very important" to future success.

We know that Delaware students perform at about the national average on standardized tests, but that shouldn't give us much comfort. Delaware is a relatively advanced state and should be far better than average, and almost everyone concedes that today's national average isn't much of a target anyway.

And speaking of average performance, we're not only concerned about our "C" and "D" students; our "A" and "B" students must also be challenged to their limit.

Now, it's not fair to blame all of the problems on the schools. Many of these discomforting trends have their roots in changes outside the schools' jurisdiction -- increasing crime and violence in our communities, reduced parental involvement, family breakdown, more teenagers working after school, substance abuse and so forth. About one in five Delaware children lives in poverty, and kindergarten teachers estimate that about two of five Delaware children aren't ready to start school.

Remember also that only some 20 percent of a child's waking hours between kindergarten and twelfth grade are spent in school. So we need to work with parents, who have a major responsibility here, and to collaborate with other agencies to prepare our children. But while schools may not have caused many of these problems, they still have to deal with their effects. We can't throw up our hands, but at the same time we must recognize how much we expect from our educators today.

In short, the situation comes down to this: Our world has changed, but our schools haven't. It's time that they do . . . but in a measured and reasoned way.

Where to Begin the Education Reform?

But how to proceed? Where to start? This is a complex problem, and there are many things we need to do. For example, nothing is more fundamental than a safe and supportive learning environment. Discipline, order, decorum and freedom from drugs and violence are prerequisites for learning. Those few chronic troublemakers must be removed from the classroom and taught in an alternative setting where they do not interfere with those who want to learn and where they can receive the help or guidance they need. Thanks to new state legislation, there are now provisions for such alternative school settings.

But how do we assure that all Delaware children reach their full academic potential and are prepared to enter college or the work force in the 21st century? How do we raise the levels of academic performance?

Delaware has a sound strategy to do this. It is entitled "New Directions for Education in Delaware," and it consists of three parts. First, kids must have the knowledge and skills which the times will require -- the basics for the 21st century. We are now defining those expectations, which we refer to as standards. Second, we must be able to measure, in a fair and accurate way, whether students meet those standards. We call that assessments. You may think of it as testing. Third, we must provide the best teaching, backed up by training, technology and other forms of support, so that the necessary learning can take place. We call this capacity building.

I'll say a few words about each aspect of New Directions -- standards, assessment and capacity building.

(1) Standards

The basic building blocks of New Directions are academic standards which outline what students need to know and be able to do in various subjects and at various grade levels. Those standards will replace the minimum competencies in reading, writing and math that Delaware, and most other states, adopted a decade ago. These minimum competencies were designed to be reached by eighth grade and were thought to be sufficient for a student to graduate. Thus, while many students took more challenging courses, some students receive diplomas without ever having taken a high-school level core course.

The new standards will be must more demanding and will require all students to solve real-world problems and to explain the reasoning and strategies they have used. Whereas the minimum competencies required students to read scale drawings, for example, or identify a right angle, the proposed math standards might require students to use this knowledge to solve real problems and to present the results in writing, orally and visually.

These standards, which will cover such areas as vocabulary, history, economics and energy, will benefit our children in several important ways. Students will learn more, and there will be the same high standards for all students. The standards will be more consistent from one school to another. Teachers will have a better idea what their students are supposed to learn.

Over the past 30 months, some two hundred Delaware teachers with more than 3,000 years of relevant classroom experience, aided by school administrators, subject matter experts and members of our business community, have provided the leadership in developing the proposed content standards in four academic areas: mathematics; science; English language arts; and social studies (which incorporates civics, economics, geography and history). Standards for other content areas will come later (see Figure 1).

An extensive process to seek expert and public review of the draft standards has been implemented statewide between October 1994 and March 1995 (see Figure 2). Thousands of copies of each draft standards document have been distributed as part of an extensive public review process. The State Board of Education will act on the proposed standards at its June (1995) meeting.

Wayne Gretzky once was asked what made him such a great hockey player. Because he said, "I go where the puck is going to be, not where it is."

The standards will be challenging but achievable, based on where students will need to be, not where they are today. Because these standards are more rigorous, it's likely that many students won't meet them right away. When that happens, we must have the courage to stay the course. The answer can't be to lower the standards. Rather, we'll have to increase our efforts to help students make progress over time.

Now, we need to reflect on this comprehensive and inclusive strategy used to develop Delaware's first sets of standards for Math and Science. Obviously, this function both requires and needs statewide and national leadership and should not be deferred to each school alone. These challenging academic standards require a greater emphasis on "teaching and learning" which is at the core of the national education goals reform strategy.

FIGURE 1

FOUR NEW DIRECTIONS CURRICULUM FRAMEWORKS COMMISSIONS

- **Mathematics**
- **Science**
- **English/Language Arts**
- **Social Studies/History/Geography**

Future Commissions:

- **Fine/PerformingArts**
- **Vocational Education**
- **International Languages**
- **Health & Physical Education**

FIGURE 2

Review of the Curriculum Standards

Delaware's four Curriculum Framework Commissions are beginning their third year of work in defining what it is that students should know and be able to do in mathematics, science, English/language arts, and history/geography/social studies. After each Commission agrees on an initial draft of its proposed standards, that draft will be published and widely disseminated for review and feedback. Once the feedback is synthesized, the Commissions will revise and edit their documents before they are presented to the State Board of Education in June 1995 for approval.

The review process will occur in five stages:

1. Expert Review. Each Commission has consulted a number of subject matter experts within Delaware and across the country to provide feedback to the Commissions on their initial drafts.

2. Educator Review. Delaware educators in general will begin their review of the standards during fall 1994 (i.e., mathematics and science in September - November) and English/Language Arts and Social Studies/History/ Geography/Civics/Economics in November-January). Discussion sessions are planned for local board members, local superintendents, district and campus administrators, teachers and teacher aides, district and campus support staffs, the Department of Public Instruction staff, the Professional Standards Council, representatives from Delaware's colleges and universities, the PTA, etc. Educators will have several weeks to review the draft standards and provide their feedback to the Commissions.

3. Public Review. The Public Review process will occur, beginning in January 1995, with briefings of several groups of state-level leaders, including the Governor and his staff and Cabinet, legislators, as well as a number of other organizations. There will be a kick-off event to signal the beginning of the Public Review in January, followed by a series of County Forums, and those followed by presentations to smaller groups of interested citizens across the state. All Delaware citizens will be invited to become well informed about the proposed standards and to provide suggestions for their improvement to the Commissions.

4. Commission Review, Synthesis and Revision. The fourth stage will be conducted by the Commissions. They will review, synthesize, and consider all the received suggestions. They will then make necessary revisions and conduct another abbreviated review process. This work will be complete by May 1995.

5. State Board Review and Approval. The final stage will be the review and approval of the proposed four sets of standards by the State Board of Education at the June 1995 meeting. The State Board has monitored each month the progress of the Curriculum Framework Commissions as they have gone about their work. The proposed four sets of standards will be transmitted to the General Assembly by May 15, 1995.

(2) Assessments

If you're going to establish clear and challenging standards of what students should know and be able to do, you also need a fair and effective way to measure student performance against those standards. But the tests we have now don't do that. First, they compare a student's performance to that of other students rather than against a performance standard. We need to know whether Johnny or Sue can do algebra, not whether they can do it as well as Margaret or Steven.

Second, the tests we have been using -- primarily multiple choice tests -- don't measure the ability to use skills and knowledge to solve real-world problems. We don't live in a multiple-choice world. We have to reason problems through on our own -- or in a group -- and arrive at solutions.

To get us started, students have begun to take so-called "interim assessments". These determine where students perform today so we can chart our progress and to identify areas where students need extra help (see Figure 3). These interim assessments do not affect whether a student passes a course or graduates.

(3) Capacity Building

So we must define the knowledge and skills kids need and be able to measure their progress. But for effective teaching and learning to take place, we must also strengthen our classroom support system. Teachers need additional support to make the most of the new standards and assessments, and as business discovered long ago, such training is a wise investment. Technology can be an effective tool to help children learn, but here again teachers need to be trained in how to use it.

We can also support teachers by identifying the very best teaching practices, wherever they exist, and making them known to all Delaware teachers. When New Directions is fully implemented, we expect to see more cooperative and group learning and less lecturing on the teacher's part. We expect to see abstract concepts related to items students already understand. We expect learning to be both more difficult and more fun. But again, this is new to many teachers, and we must help them with the transition.

FIGURE 3

Performance Assessment Achievement - Grade 10

The State Board of Education established student performance standards in Reading, Writing and Mathematics for the Interim Assessment period, 1993-1995. The school's results for 1993 and 1994 are reported by the percentage of students who scored in each of three performance levels: 1) Meets or Exceeds the Standard; 2) Approaches the Standard; and 3) Considerably Below the Standard. The explanation of what these levels mean is on the inside pages.

The graphs below present this school's results on th Performance Assessments, when students were asked to open-ended questions, write a composition on an assigne solve realistic math problems. The 1994 results are also re gender and race. Similar assessments will be given in 199 the Fall, each school will review the results of these asses set improvement goals.

ACHIEVEMENT BY SCHOOL – 1993 VS. 1994

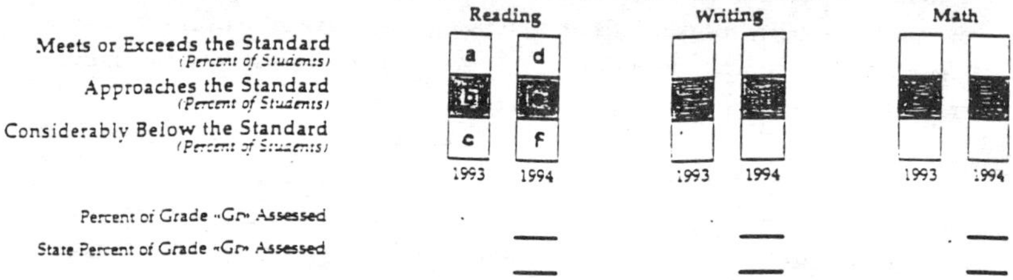

ACHIEVEMENT BY GENDER – 1994

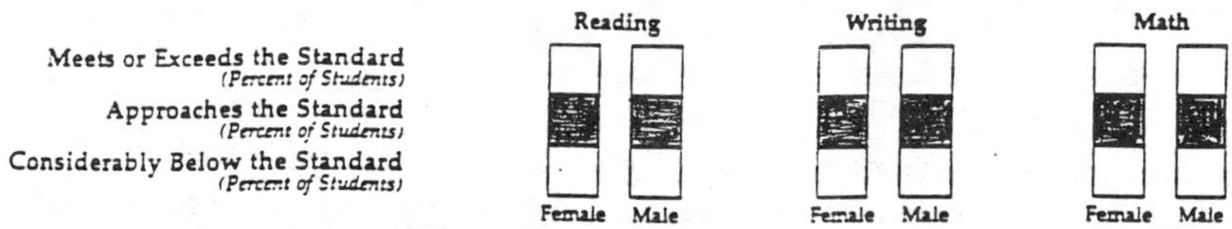

ACHIEVEMENT BY RACIAL & ETHNIC CATEGORIES – 199

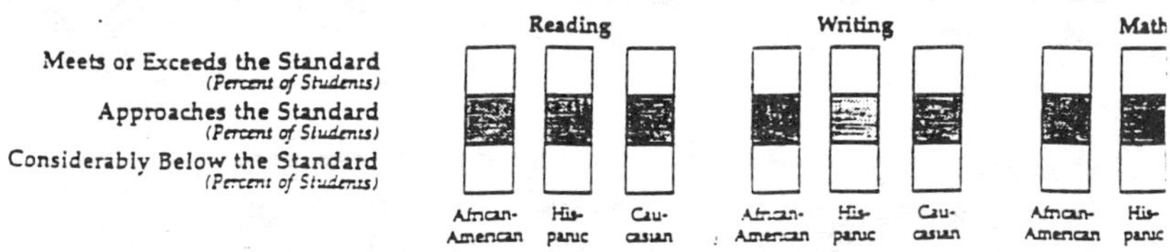

In brief, that's what New Directions is about: Creating standards of what kids should know and be able to do, developing assessments to measure their progress and putting the necessary support mechanisms into place so that schools and districts can build the programmatic and instructional systems that they deem appropriate to achieve the standard.

New Directions attempts to incorporate the best features of an education reform strategy that balances both "bottom up" ownership and "top down" leadership.

Our standards based reform is about making central those elements of the system that deserve to be standardized, but which are not in our current educational systems, namely:

- expectations and standards,
- performance measures and assessments,
- benchmarks of performance (Let's stop the grade inflation; let's put meaning and clarity back so an A will be an A);

and, about decentralizing what often has been centralized, but should not have been in our current system, namely:

- curriculum,
- instruction,
- teaching practices.

The latter elements need to be the domain of local determination. As Figure 4 illustrates, we in the New Directions Partnership have worked hard at clarifying respective roles and responsibilities. At the heart of Delaware's education reform agenda is a basic and essential commitment to staff development. A distinguishing feature should be the creation of extensive opportunities for educators to deeply reflect on their practice. As the Curriculum Framework Commission members will attest, the processes of designing, developing and putting in place our Delaware standards qualifies as among the best staff development for our premier educators. Thus, our reform efforts must have a catalytic impact on the system, rather than a perfunctory exercise in selecting someone else's work.

FIGURE 4

CLARIFYING STATE AND LOCAL ROLES AND RESPONSIBILITIES

Just as we are asking Delaware's students and educators to stretch and reach for higher standards, we must be prepared to ask no less of the State of Delaware and its Department of Public Instruction.

"New Directions for Education in Delaware" is the state's standards-based approach to education reform that calls for institution of challenging academic standards of performance for all students and for the regular monitoring of progress by students and schools against these appropriate benchmarks. These two key components of the New Directions reform effort have been referred to by the State Superintendent as the pieces of bread of "the sandwich"— the top and bottom. We all recognize that to improve the academic performance of Delaware's public school students, we must promote the "meat of the sandwich"—better teaching and student learning at the local level.

New Directions partners (the State Board of Education, local boards of education, the Delaware Business/Public Education Council, the public higher education presidents, the Delaware State Education Association, the General Assembly and the Governor) are committed to creating world class public school systems in Delaware that will achieve our vision of excellence and equity for all students.

For the five years of the New Directions Partnerships (ie.,FY '93-FY '97), four permanent educational priorities have been established to guide state and local educational reform efforts in Delaware: Standards and Curriculum. Assessments and Instruction, Capacity Building and Local Implementation, and Partnerships. Each has complementary statewide and local-level roles and responsibilities and all four are essential long term to the success of New Directions.

Priorities *State Roles*	*Local Roles*
Standards Establish statewide expectations for content and for student performance.	**Curriculum** Develop and implement curriculum and materials that will ensure all students are challenged academically and have an opportunity to meet or exceed the standards.
Assessments Develop and administer statewide assessments to evaluate progress of each school and student in meeting or exceeding the standards.	**Instruction** Develop and implement teaching practices and on-going assessment. that will ensure that all students meet or exceed the standards.
Capacity Building Provide leadership both to identify and secure the resources for professional development and system enhancements and to remove statutory and regulatory barriers to quality to ensure that the activities of New Directions can be implemented so all children can succeed	**Local Implementation** Utilize state and local resources for professional development and system enhancements to provide programs and services that ensure that all students meet or exceed the standards.
Partnerships Develop and maintain partnerships with key constituents to ensure the support of New Directions statewide.	**Partnerships** Develop and maintain partnerships with key constituents to ensure the support of New Directions community wide.

A Scientific Example

Let me provide an example of how this fits together. I'm going to take the proposed life processes science standard that deals with something called enzymes. Now, you may have gotten through life pretty well with little or no knowledge of enzymes, but enzymes are all around us, and today's high school student should have at least a basic knowledge of what they are and how they can be affected by such factors as temperature and acidity.

To acquire this understanding children might use models to observe how enzymes interact under certain conditions. Teachers would develop an assortment of enzyme tasks, with students working in small groups and designing their own tests. At one table students might investigate how acidity or alkalinity affects the enzyme contained in human saliva. Another group might investigate whether hard water affects the ability of enzymes in detergents to remove protein stains.

A few Delaware teachers have tried such approaches and are very excited about their experience. It is also important to recognize that a number of the elements of the New Directions reform agenda have received high levels of support from all of the Delaware citizens recently surveyed as part of the 1994 Public Poll on the Condition of Education in Delaware are conducted by the Delaware Education Research and Development Center. Let's see what the people of Delaware want:

• supporting training and development of professionals in the schools	89%
• establishing statewide standards for students	88%
• giving teachers more authority for decisions within the schools	86%
• holding schools accountable by reporting test scores for each student	83%
• holding school districts accountable by reporting test scores for each district.	82%

Thus, our education reform agenda is directly addressing what our Delaware public wants us to do.

92-107 O - 95 - 2

State Deregulations Efforts To Date

We also recognize that the core contribution of New Directions can only build a solid foundation or platform for centering the Delaware reform agenda. Simultaneously, the State Board has been moving ahead to support and prepare for the systemic demands. The State Board of Education has begun to remove possible "landmines" or constraints facing the New Directions partners. We've had a short term and long term strategy.

There are five recent examples of State Board actions to address identified statutory and regulatory barriers that impede the implementation of New Directions:

1. Removed state required "minimum competency" recordkeeping and reporting requirements;

2. Removed potential state control of textbook adoption;

3. Removed potential state control of curriculum and instructional materials;

4. Approved district request for the creation of a high school "open enrollment" system to allow parents and students to choose among four district high schools; and

5. Approved district request for a school calendar modification to provide two additional days for staff inservice education to support districtwide restructuring efforts.

Moreover, the Governor's Education Improvement Commission (EIC) has specifically been charged to bring forward proposals and strategies for:

- decentralizing decision making
- deregulating the school system
- holding schools accountable for their results related to student performance.

The EIC is also identifying opportunities to improve the efficiency and effectiveness of Delaware's current annual public education expenditures to that the recommendations the Gap Analysis can be implemented in a revenue-neutral basis.

Summary

As you think about the need for change and New Directions, keep this thought in mind. This year's seventh grade class will graduate from high school in June of the year 2000 – the 21st century. They are already more than half way through their basic education. Are we adequately preparing them for what they will face?

For the sake of these children, and all children . . . for the sake of our economy . . . and for the sake of our democracy, we must equip our young people with the skills needed for the world of today and tomorrow. All interested Delawareans, whether involved in education or not, can make a meaningful contribution by participating in the standards review and in the work of your local school.

Let's remember the basics of New Directions:

- New Directions is about the **academic basics**:
    - tough and challenging standards in core academic subjects of mathematics, science, English language arts and social studies;
    - a shared vision of excellence and equity for all students by the partners as the platform or foundation for education restructuring;
- New Directions will give **local communities** the power to shape their education programs and systems:
    - diversity and flexibility in designing and implementing educational programs and systems to be located at the local level;
    - deregulation and school empowerment;

- New Directions is committed to supporting the **continuous improvement** of our students, staff, schools and systems and to holding ourselves **accountable** for demonstrated progress against the high standards over time:

  - flexibility and openness;
  - greater coherence in reform strategies.

I hope you agree with me that constructive change is needed and that Delaware has an exciting and sensible plan to make that happen. After all, few things in this life are more important than launching our young people successfully.

SUBCOMMITTEE ON OVERSIGHT AND INVESTIGATIONS
U. S. HOUSE OF REPRESENTATIVES
WASHINGTON, DC

SUPPLEMENTARY ORAL STATEMENT*

ACCOMPANYING

PREVIOUSLY SUBMITTED TESTIMONY

ON

"A STATE PERSPECTIVE ON EDUCATIONAL STANDARDS:

THE DELAWARE EXPERIENCE"

by

Pascal D. Forgione, Jr., Ph.D.
State Superintendent of Public Instruction
Department of Public Instruction
P. O. Box 1402
Dover, DE 19901
(302) 739-4601
(Fax) (302) 739-4654

March 22, 1995

* My testimony and comments today represent my personal views.

Good morning.

Representative Hoekstra, members of the Subcommittee and ladies and gentlemen. I am Dr. Pat Forgione, State Superintendent of Public Instruction for the State of Delaware. I have served in my current capacity for some 40 months. Prior to that appointment, I spent one year in Washington as the first Executive Director of the National Education Goals Panel. Before that I spent 12 years with the Connecticut State Department of Education in a senior leadership position.

I am pleased to be invited to participate this morning in this important and timely discussion on education standards. I am sure that my participation is intended to offer a concrete and ground level view of the realities that state and local districts are confronting in this important and hard educational improvement work to raise academic expectations for our public schools and to achieve enhanced academic performance by all our students, the nation's most precious resource.

I have submitted a written testimony that details Delaware's education reform initiative, titled "New Directions for Education in Delaware", which is in its third year of a five-year reform plan. I should note that this is truly a partnership activity with each of our nineteen Delaware school districts contributing financially to support the reform at $5.00 per student. Since there are about 100,000 students statewide, this has generated over one-half million dollars from the local districts for each of the first three years. This amount is being matched by the Delaware business community (i.e., the Business Public/ Education Council). The State Board of Education also is contributing $7.00 per student, or $700,000 per year. Thus, our education reform partnership in Delaware means something concrete in terms of our partners' willingness to make a personal investment in this important standards development work. I'll return to this theme later in my presentation.

My accompanying written testimony outlines a practical, common sense approach that my state has chosen to launch to prepare our young children for college, for the world at work and for life in the 21st Century, which is only five years away. The accompanying paper provides a rich description of the actual experiences that my state has encountered in our efforts in two key activities: (a) to build deep and broad agreement statewide on more rigorous academic standards in the core disciplines of mathematics, science, English language arts and social studies, (which is defined as civics, economics, geography and history); and (b) to design and implement new assessments or testing systems that will regularly monitor the progress that Delaware public schools and students make in achieving our shared academic goals. Fortunately, Delaware's approach is reflective of, and largely compatible to, at least some three dozen other states nationally that are proceeding to implement standards-based education reform initiatives. This policy move to standards-based education is a dramatic shift from the previous focus on inputs and processes to an emphasis on academic results. In addition, the development of challenging academic standards is a foundational activity that is a prerequisite to our fulfilling the joint agreement and commitment that the fifty governors and states endorsed in 1989 at the Charlottesville Education Summit as part of the creation of the National Education Goal. In particular this involves two goals: student achievement and citizenship, and science and mathematics.

In the brief few minutes I have this morning, I wish to bring out some of the major features of Delaware's standards-based education reform. I will also offer a set of specific comments related to the Education America Act -- Goals 2000, Title II, the remarks from which I will submit as a supplemental statement following this presentation.

There are three major points that I need to make up front regarding our national and interstate commitment to educational standards. First, let us remember why we are all about this important work of enhancing academic standards of our schools. You will notice I am wearing a lapel pin that reminds me each day of what my central mission is as a public education official -- Children First. We need to continually remind ourselves of our collective raison d'être. There is a needed federal investment in our children's development and this investment must be closely coordinated with state and local efforts – Children First. Second, we have chosen to begin this challenging work with the national education goals. At the heart of these goals is our focus on academic achievement of all children. Wayne Gretsky once was asked what made him such a great hockey player. Because, he said, "I go where the puck is going to be, not where it is." So, also, this nation deserves a set of "stretch" national goals and accompanying standards. National is different from federal. We should be pleased at this point that our initial intergovernmental efforts have been bipartisan, consensual and leadership-oriented. We must reaffirm our shared commitment to the national education goals and support the multi-state momentum under way to implement standards-based strategies related to the national education goals. And third, there is an appropriate and vital federal role in supporting educational standards.

A federal role, I believe, is necessary and needs to be crafted with emphasis on: voluntary national standards, with multiple models and rich examples; and flexibility in supporting the directions chosen by the states and localities. I would support the Subcommittee's fine tuning elements of Title II of Goals 2000 to remove such provisions, as NESIC, the certification of standards, and the opportunity to learn standards. However, I strongly support a number of provisions of Title II. I also support the use of the National Education Goals Panel as an appropriate body to conduct the needed "review and comment" function on emerging voluntary national and state standards.

Moreover, I wish the Subcommittee to know that Delaware's hard and challenging work to develop standards over the past two years has been impacted largely in a positive manner and has been meaningfully informed by what is happening with a number of national standards development projects. So, also, in the future, the potential benefits of what happens with the goals panel's work on building indicators and on monitoring progress toward the national goals will be very useful to states as we develop our own accountability and support systems. To date, I have seen no evidence of any instance where the work being done at the national level has rigidly dictated or negatively impaired Delaware's curriculum framework and standards development work. Delaware's four draft standards documents are presently under a six-month review process by experts, educators and the general public (see page seven of my accompanying testimony document). Figure 2 describes the five stages of this review process which will be completed by June, 1995.

Let me now give you two examples that I believe illustrate some of the tensions that we are facing at the state and local level. First, in science, the National Research Council's work on the national science education standards has a strong and direct relationship with Delaware's work. It was extremely valuable for our science leadership team to come over and interact with the NRC staff. I believe we were able to influence the national group to give more attention to certain areas, such as solutions. So it was a "give and take" process. Currently, Delaware's science standards commission and the NSF-funded Delaware Systemic Initiative are reviewing the national draft science standards to look for alignment and gaps. I urge you not to extend any cutoff of federal funding to such voluntary standards efforts that have been arrived at by grassroots consensus building. Standards, such as these and the National Council for the Teachers of Mathematics, represent essential resources for states and localities as they move forward to align the development of their own curriculum to improving the teaching and learning in the core national goals areas.

A second example is illustrative of why states need an active, purposeful and appropriately focused federal investment strategy. Let me relate Delaware's attempt to analyze statewide our science curriculum practices which are currently incoherent and of generally poor quality. We wish to move the teaching of science in Delaware to world class status. In the winter of 1993 during a visit to Japan, Dr. Joe Miller, a co-chair of the Delaware science commission and a senior vice president with DuPont, secured a copy of the Japanese national science standards which we had translated into English through the DuPont library system. Over the past year this resource has caused our science commission to reflect more deeply. Why do the Japanese introduce this concept before that one? Why is the Japanese scope and sequence different for a particular area? This volume has proven to be a valuable resource as our science commission moved forward to define what Delaware students should know and be able to do in science and to benchmark our scientific expectations against the best performing education systems in the world. But should Delaware's future be conditioned on such fortunate circumstances? I believe not. A strategic federal investment in the development and dissemination of such materials would be an absolute asset and a prerequisite to our assisting states and districts in making the most of our current standards and assessments development work.

Moreover, I see three particularly appropriate federal research roles: (a) supporting the development of performance assessments for specific content areas by consortia of states, especially in underdeveloped areas such as science; (b) sponsoring research on linking state assessments to national and international assessments; and (c) fostering international benchmarking studies. These are three purposeful and unique research and development activities that would pay rich returns to states through a federal education investment in research and development.

In conclusion, I respectfully ask, on behalf of my colleague states, that you please stay the course and do not dismantle Goals 2000. Please fulfill the partnership responsibility inherent in the national education goals and continue to work in concert with colleague states as part of our shared commitment to effect enhanced student academic performance across the nation. States and districts cannot do this essential work alone. Without a focused and strategic federal education investment we will likely be unable to insure excellence and equity for all of America's children.

Thank you.

Chairman HOEKSTRA. Thank you. Ms. Cheney.

STATEMENT OF HON. LYNNE CHENEY, AMERICAN ENTERPRISE INSTITUTE, WASHINGTON, DC

Ms. CHENEY. Thank you very much. I've been sitting here listening to the conversation and, as I've listened to the conversation going on today, I've been struck by what seems to me is a certain confusion.

We're talking about two different kinds of standards, and I don't think we've made that clear. The ones that I think Mr. Cunningham and Mr. Hoekstra held up are national standards. They were developed with the idea that there would be an entity called NESIC that would approve these standards, and then they would thereby influence the States, and we would have standards across the Nation that were relatively the same.

Think of this as the French model. You can call it the Japanese model, if you want, but it's the model that is used in France. It's the model that's used in Japan. You have one standard that is across the Nation, and you can develop the national assessment based on that.

I think that has influenced a lot of thinking in so far as the development of standards has gone. It certainly influenced my thinking. It was the history standards that brought me up short, and it told me we need to think of another model. That is the wrong model. The French model, the Japanese model, is wrong for us.

We are too big a country. It is too dangerous in this country—and unconstitutional besides—to have the Federal Government in a role where they can dictate a set of standards that will influence the Nation as a whole.

I would like to congratulate Mr. Hoekstra and Chairman Goodling as well, for introducing legislation that will hopefully get rid of NESIC, so that we won't be in a position to serve high standards like that—the history standards, of course, trouble me most—that will impact the Nation as a whole. The French model. The Japanese model.

These, I have here, standards that have been developed in Virginia, or the standards of Delaware that Dr. Forgione was kind enough to tell us about. Think of that as the German model. This is a different kind of standard entirely in terms of its provenance, as we would say in our history, in terms of where it comes from.

It comes from the states. This is the way they do it in Germany. The different German states develop these standards. And then they have a coordinating body of the Ministers of Education of each state that gets together. It has hardly any power at all.

When I visited Germany, I was still thinking in the French and Japanese models, and I wanted them to tell me—oh, we let the states develop the standards, and then we get together in this federal body, the Convention of Land Ministers, and, boy, do we put those standards through a grinder and make sure that they're all quite comparable with one another in all of the types—and they would never tell me that, and it's because I was still thinking in that old paradigm. I kept getting frustrated that they wouldn't say that. But they would say, no, this body doesn't have a whole lot of power, but we do sit there, and we kind of acknowledge among ourselves that, in Bavaria, they do give harder exams than they do in Berlin, and this word gradually makes its way across the country as a whole.

This is so much the better model for us. We are simply not, in this country, given our Constitution, given the breadth and the width and the size of this Nation, we are not suited for the Japanese model. We are not suited for the French model.

There's an old saying about the French model, that you can look at your watch and be sure that a student in third grade in Lyon studying exactly the same thing a French student in third grade in Marseilles or Normandy is studying. That's not for us. We're not that kind of Nation.

We need to think of these—these—as our standards, these standards that are being developed in the States. I am so pleased to see these Virginia standards. They are quite wonderful. They are still at the stage that Dr. Forgione is talking about. They are going to be distributed around the State. They will be subject to a lot of comment. And then the citizens of Virginia will have the standards they have developed for their students.

It seems to me that the National Education Goals Panel might be the right body for coordination. You know, that's where the standards can come, and you can look and you can see how they sit, and you can discuss how they might be different, but the idea of having the National Education Goals Panel be given, for example, the history standards, even be given the math standards, even be given the English standards, and for them to be able to say, well, these make it and these don't, I've got to tell you, especially after the experience of the history standards, I do not think this is a good idea.

For the National Education Goals Panel to be coordinating, yes. For it to be reviewing and certifying and approving, I don't think so. Partly because—Mr. Cunningham, I thought you made a wonderful point—if we hadn't had—I am convinced if we had not had the election in 1994, there had not been a change in the majority leadership of this body and the other body, I am convinced that the history standards would have been certified by the National Education Standards and Improvement Council, and we would today be living with that result.

We should not be in a situation where an election can make a change like that—not an election from Democrat to Republican or Republican to Democrat—that's just wrong. We shouldn't be in that kind of situation at all.

So, let me just give you a couple of examples of why I am concerned that standards that are developed on that French model, that Japanese model, go to any sort of government body and be approved.

I've heard a lot about how wonderful the math standards are. I've got here just a few pages. I think there are some things in here that are very worrisome. For example, the math standards have sort of—you know how the newspapers run these things, what's in this year and what's out this year—well, the math standards have in them what's in now in math, and what's out. And, frankly, I don't think a lot of citizens and a lot of your States are going to be real pleased with what's in and what's out on the math standards.

For example, among the things that are out, complex paper and pencil computations. Oh, really? That's out now? Long division. Oh, really? That's out. Paper and pencil fraction computation.

Now, do you really think that the citizens in your State don't think your kids ought to learn to do fractions with paper and pencil? But I suspect that if you get a National Education Goals Panel in the business of approving these things, that this will be considered some kind of a detail. These will go through. They will have national impact in a way that they shouldn't.

You're going to have trouble at the State level, too. My friend, Irving Crystal—and I'm just going to be so frank and honest with you today—my friend, Irving Crystal, has an iron law of education reform. He says, any—and, Mr. Shanker, I especially apologize to you because you do not fit the stereotype I'm about to perpetuate—any education reform approved of by the education establishment is worse than doing nothing at all.

The National Education Goals Panel, I am afraid if it sets up an approving body, it will be an approving body that is the education establishment, and that's why things like this, what's in and what's out in math, will go sailing right through.

The education establishment is also very powerful at the State level, but there's something else that goes on there, and that's the fact that citizens at the State level have their kids in a school there, and they care very much, and they are willing to stand up and fight. You don't get a real concern about what happens when you have these things at the national level.

So, I think it's very important, as we move forward, that you at least consider my recommendation that we think of ourselves along the line of a German model, with any governmental body simply a governmental body that is there to coordinate, a body that is there to give mutual advice, but not set in place any sort of government entity that has the power to say, this is good, this is bad, and with that power, to give whatever is approved an amazing half-life that we may well regret. Thank you for the opportunity to testify.

[The prepared statement of Ms. Cheney follows:]

Testimony of Lynne V. Cheney, W. H. Brady, Jr. Distinguished Fellow, American Enterprise Institute; Chairman, National Endowment for the Humanities, 1986-1993, before the House Education and Economic Opportunities Subcommittee on Oversight and Investigations on March 22, 1995.

During the past decade the case for national standards in core academic subjects has been presented thoughtfully and clearly. No doubt you will hear most of these arguments repeated today. I am familiar with them because I used to make many of them myself. They seemed eminently sensible.

The arguments typically go like this: Our children are not achieving at high levels, partly because we are not expecting enough of them. We should do what other developed nations do: that is, set out what we expect, develop standards in core academic subjects, and then test to see if students have acquired the knowledge and skills we think are important.

Over the past several years such arguments have convinced many and have led to the funding of proposed national standards in core academic subjects by the federal government under both the Bush and Clinton administrations.

The results are now in on the process of setting national standards in education. Let us examine some of the specifics.

The proposed national standards in United States and world history developed by the History Center at UCLA have proved to be an utter disaster. Although the authors of the history standards promised in their application to the National Endowment for the Humanities to build the standards on previously published, highly-regarded work, the standards that were produced bear little relationship to it. They present a grim and biased view of our history and of the history of Western Civilization.

Who would have predicted, at the beginning of the process in 1991, that the proposed national standards in history would be condemned by the United States Senate by a vote of 99-1? Senator Joseph Lieberman of Connecticut said the standards would give our children a "warped and negative view" of America and the West. He is right. The history standards are seriously flawed from start to finish, and no amount of revision will "fix" them.

The United States history standards imply that Joseph McCarthy (mentioned 19 times in the standards) is more important to our nation's story than George Washington (mentioned twice) or Robert E. Lee (mentioned not at all). Some of America's (and the world's) greatest achievements in science are ignored. Alexander Graham Bell, the Wright Brothers, Thomas Edison, Albert Einstein, Jonas Salk, and Neil Armstrong are never mentioned in the U.S. history standards, although the standards do contain references to Roseanne Arnold and Bart Simpson.

The world history standards denigrate the role of Western civilization and glorify the achievements of the non-West. Reading the world history standards one would think that sexism and ethnocentrism arose in the West, when Western civilization has in fact led the way in condemning unjust treatment of women and encouraging curiosity about other cultures. Reading the world history standards one would become familiar with the urban complexities of Aztec civilization, but not with that culture's pervasive practice of human sacrifice. Reading the world history standards one would conclude that the Cold War was primarily a contest between two morally equivalent "superpowers," not a struggle between liberal democracy and totalitarianism.

The proposed national standards in English/language arts, currently in draft form, present another case study of serious problems with the national standards process. To begin with, one should ask why the standards are called English/language arts, instead of simply English, as the President and the governors envisioned at the National Education Summit in 1989. The reason is that the term "English" unlike the concept "language arts" implies that the English language is more important for students in the United States than other languages. Because this is anathema to many professionals in the field the standards are stuck with the jargon-laden term, "English/language arts."

The English standards also seem to have been infected with the virus of postmodernism. In a draft, they define literacy as "an active process of constructing meaning." We have students graduating from our high schools who can't read bus schedules and we are proposing to fix this by defining literacy as "the construction of meaning"? Literacy means that they should be able to tell that the bus is coming at 3:00, not that they can invent its arrival time.

Why have we had these tremendous problems trying to develop national education standards? I believe it is because of the current state of our universities, and of our educational and cultural institutions. The academy in general, and the humanities in particular, have become highly politicized. Many academics no longer see their purpose as pursuing truth through objective inquiry, but in achieving political and social transformation through whatever means lead to those ends.

Although I once thought it possible for this tendency to be overcome and for sensible standards to be developed, I no longer think so--and the history and English/language arts standards are cases in point.

I know that there are people who think that developing national standards will make us more competitive in world economic markets. But I believe this is misguided. How, for example, would the flawed history and English/language arts standards help

America's global competitiveness? If anything they will set us back. I can't imagine, for example, that many of our competitors are advancing history curricula for students that portray their country and culture as deeply flawed.

Where do we go from here? Certainly, Congressman Goodling, Congressman Hoekstra and the other co-sponsors of H.R. 1045 are to be commended for their determination to eliminate the National Education Standards and Improvement Council (NESIC) and the so-called Opportunity to Learn Standards (OTL).

Assuming that NESIC will be eliminated, the Subcommittee posed the following question as a potential topic for discussion at today's hearing: what is needed to support standards-based reform in a post-NESIC world? Let me briefly try to answer this.

In the broadest sense, what is needed is devolution and decentralization. The election of November 1994 signaled, in large part, a desire to move decision making from the federal to the state and local level. States, localities, and schools should set their own education standards without interference from the federal government.

We should not have a single set of "national" standards, nor do we need any federal body, including the National Education Goals Panel, putting an imprimatur or good housekeeping seal of approval on any set of standards: national, state, or local. And we certainly do not need a quasi-official body, funded by private foundations (and thus without any public accountability or sunshine provisions), to develop a "consensus" of subject area specialists, who would then put their own "quasi-official" stamp of approval on national and state standards.

We should move from national standards to state standards--from systemic reform to marketplace-based reform--from a consensus-based process to a competitive model.

Some believe that the states are incapable of developing their own standards without federal direction and without considerable costs. I don't believe that. This past weekend I reviewed the state of Virginia's proposed new education standards. They are eminently sensible and academically solid. They are, in my opinion, more rigorous and objective than many of the proposed national standards that I have seen.

I understand that the cost of the Virginia standards project is around $250,000. A Governor's commission of volunteers including elected officials, lay people, parents, teachers, and scholars worked with local school divisions and the state board of education.

In many areas of American public life the 104th Congress is

returning power to the states and localities. The process of setting rigorous education standards is another area where devolution and decentralization make sense.

Chairman HOEKSTRA. Thank you. Mr. Shanker.

STATEMENT OF MR. AL SHANKER, PRESIDENT, AMERICAN FEDERATION OF TEACHERS, WASHINGTON, DC

Mr. SHANKER. Mr. Chairman, Members of the committee, thank you very much for this opportunity to testify.

I think it's important that we all recognize that we're not dealing with just one other piece of legislation. In my view, the structure which is set up by Goals 2000, a structure which needs some completion but, nevertheless, it's a structure without which we are not going to significantly improve our educational system.

We have seen all kinds of panaceas offered over the last 10 years, and there are a lot of them floating around now. Most of these panaceas that are proposed here don't exist anywhere else in the world, so they may or may not work, but the fact is they are all sort of rolling the dice to see if something new will work.

If we were prudent business people and, if our business started sliding, we might take a chance and do something that nobody has ever done before, but the chances are we would take a look at successful competitors and see what it is that they are doing that we are not doing.

And what our successful competitors are doing, even though they all have different school systems—the German system is different from the French system, is different from the Japanese system, is different from the Australian system—but, nevertheless, they all have certain things in common. They either have national or state standards. If you don't know where you're going, you're not going to get there, and you need a definition of that.

And they have assessment systems that are linked to those standards, so that if you study for tests and you pass the tests, you know that you've met these standards.

They have teacher training programs that are geared to preparing teachers to teach to the standards. They have textbooks that are geared to those standards. And a missing piece from Goals 2000, there are consequences for achieving or not achieving the standards.

When I was a teacher and I assigned my youngsters some homework or some project to do, six or seven kids would shout out, does it count. And, of course, what they were saying is, if that is going to be part of my grade I'm going to do the work, and if it's not part of my grade I'm not going to do the work.

Well, the youngsters in these other countries work hard to achieve these standards and to do well on the tests because they know they will not get into any college or university in the country unless they meet certain standards, or they won't get into technical schools unless they meet another set of standards, or they won't get into apprenticeship programs and, until these are eventually linked to consequences so that parents and teachers and youngsters know that working hard is an important thing and at the end of that you get rewarded, and if you're lazy and don't work hard you're not going to get the same rewards and benefits that working hard and succeeding does—that is, teaching them that they have individual responsibility. Our schools don't do that, so we need this system.

Now, we're not going to have this without a Federal role. Somebody—look, there's almost nobody in the States who knows what a world class standard looks like. If you ask people in most States to develop world class standards, they would put a bunch of teachers together and say, develop world class standards. And they sit around and look at what they did last year and say, let's do a little better. Let's make it a little harder. Let's put a little more in there. And that's viewed world class.

Very few of these places take a look at what do kids learn in the fifth grade in Germany. What do they learn in Australia. What do they learn in Japan. What do they learn in France. And if youngsters can do that kind of work in other countries, why can't they do that level of work here?

Practically nobody asks that. There's almost no literature on it. And Pat Forgione was absolutely right, he had the benefit of that Japanese translation. You need a place that's going to do that. You need a place that's going to take examinations, that's going to take textbooks, that's going to take standards and curriculum from other places, and do a technical sort of assessment and say, what this State is going to do, how does that compare with what people are doing elsewhere?

Now, that's a job that is unlikely to be done State-by-State. You need some group that has the capacity to do it. It's sort of a technical research job. It's not ideology. It's not seat-of-the-pants guesswork. It's the kind of work that Lynn Cheney started when she was with the National Endowment for the Humanities. She published a wonderful little document giving some of the questions on examinations in other countries, for college-bound students. Wonderful. It's just a sampling, and just in humanities, but that needs to be done.

Somebody needs to be able to tell Colorado, or Alabama, or New York, here's what your standards, grade-by-grade, look like in comparison to what's done elsewhere, and then you do what you want with it. That's your business in your State or your locality, but at least we are giving you that information.

Now, what are the consequences of not doing this? Well, I can tell you that right now the work that students do does not depend on standards adopted by States or by anybody else. Basically, the work that students do depends on the work that individual teacher in a classroom decides to give the students because there are very few mandates. Most of the State standards or State curriculums are guidelines. They are big, fat documents that say, select from among these things, so basically you can do what you want.

When I used to give youngsters work to do, a lot of work—because you don't learn how to write well without writing frequently, and without having someone look at what you've written, and without doing it over again, and doing it constantly, otherwise, you never get to a level where you feel comfortable doing it—when I gave that work, the youngsters would say, Mr. Shanker, you're mean. Our other teachers don't give us that much work. My sister doesn't get that much work. We're not going to do it, that's just too much. And each teacher in the United States is put in the position of individually negotiating what the curriculum is going to be with the students. Read a book that came out several years ago, called The Shopping Mall High School.

Now, that's not true in Germany or in France. A teacher can say, this is what the youngsters are learning in fourth grade throughout the country, and this is what they learned last year, and the year before, and at the end of this year you're going to have a test, which the State is providing, and I'm not your enemy, I'm not mean, I'm here to help you pass that test. It puts you in a relationship of a coach helping a youngster to reach a standard, rather than being the person who wilfully is imposing all sorts of onerous chores on the youngsters.

I think there's something else here. When we shy away from the notion of national standards, we're forgetting something. It was a Nation At Risk, and still is, and is a Nation competing with other countries, and it's also a Nation that's very mobile in terms of its population.

Education consists of building blocks. What you learn in second grade needs to have some relationship to the first grade, and the third the second. One of the reasons that American students are so far behind is that if I, as a seventh grade teacher, have no idea of what the first grade teacher did, and what the second grade teacher did, and what the third grade teacher did, then in order to teach, I have to start reviewing the first six years of work in order to make sure that my kids have the background. That review takes a tremendous amount of time, and that's why we're so far behind.

So, I know that there's great reluctance to talk about national standards, but when youngsters move from one school to another, from one district to another, from one State to another, there are schools where 60 percent of the students will move in any given year, and schools with more than that.

Now, the extent to which you say that the local school ought to determine, or the local district, you are creating a discontinuity in the education of huge numbers of youngsters. They are just going to fall behind. Or the teachers are going to have to stop what they are doing with the other youngsters, and review.

You cannot have a system that has all the mobility as this country has, without having some greater uniformity than you have at the present time.

Now, let me just say a final word about the education establishment. The education establishment doesn't want any standards. The education establishment does not want any assessments that will show the shortcomings of the system.

The education establishment fought to put opportunity to learn standards in and said that you cannot use any assessment or any consequences until every opportunity to learn a thing has been fulfilled. That's another way of saying that until every youngster has had everything right in his life up to the time of the test, you can't give him the test.

The education establishment didn't press for the goals. Now the education establishment may be compelled to accept all this, but this is not coming from the education establishment. By the way, there's a lot of looseness in the system. There's a lot of freedom. People can do what they want, and we don't know really what's happening because there aren't these standards, and there aren't assessments that really tell us anything.

This is going to put a system in place which is going to reveal a lot of things about the system. If you go out there and talk to establishment people, they're going to question if the goals are valid for everybody? Isn't each one individual? Shouldn't each teacher be able to do his or her own thing? You have creativity at the school level. Isn't this going to result in standardization? Et cetera, et cetera. You're going to get a million excuses.

This is not an establishment program. Quite the contrary. Even if you enact this and you get it out there, and have governors pushing for it, and people like Pat Forgione and others, it's going to take quite a while before there is any feeling out there that this—well, let me put it this way. This essentially deals with raising academic standards, and our schools today do not focus on anything that's academic.

The focus is on social adjustment. The focus is on self-esteem and happiness. The focus is on a whole bunch of other things. But there is not a focus on learning mathematics, or learning to read well, or to write well, or anything like that.

So, this is an antiestablishment program, and that's why I'm supporting it. And I don't think you've seen the establishment lining up out here, demanding that you have standards certified and imposed on them. Quite the contrary.

I very strongly urge that you maintain support for the structure of Goals 2000. And if you throw out NESIC, that's all right, but there needs to be someplace that looks at these standards, if the States want them looked at, and issues a report and says, well, here's how they compare with other States, here's how they compare with what's being done in other countries at those grade levels, put it out there and accompany that report with all sorts of comments from people elsewhere.

I certainly will want to comment on them. I'm sure that Ms. Cheney will. I'm sure that most of the people here will. Put that package together and put it out there, and let the people in the States look at that document and give it whatever weight it deserves. Then if you've got something like these national history standards, you'll have a package of comments out there which will raise enough questions so that nobody will adopt them, if they're in their right mind. But it's a lot better to have that public debate about national standards, than to have those same standards creep in the schools systems around the country, without anybody knowing about them or without anybody debating them. Thank you.

[The prepared statement of Mr. Shanker follows:]

TESTIMONY OF ALBERT SHANKER

Mr. Chairman and members of the Subcommittee, my name is Albert Shanker, president of the 875,000 members of the American Federation of Teachers (AFT). I appreciate this invitation to speak to you about education standards. This issue has been a central preoccupation of mine, and I am proud to say that the AFT has been an ardent advocate of the movement to establish clear and rigorous academic standards for what students should know and be able to do as a result of their education. I believe that standards are the lever for turning around the mediocre performance of our education system, both public and private, and that this is a vital national interest. So let me be blunt about my views:

If Congress shoots down a federal role in the effort to establish voluntary national and state academic standards that are benchmarked to the most competitive in the world, it will destroy the standards movement in all but name only.

It will not be an affirmation of our tradition of state responsibility for and local control of education; it will be a rejection of the explicit request for help on standards most of our states and districts have made and a repudiation of the historic national interest in education.

It will not be a vote of confidence that Americans' ingenuity will enable us to reach the national education goals on our own; it will be tantamount to repealing those goals.

It will not be a rejection of standardization; it will be a rejection of models of excellence.

It will not save money; it will ensure that this nation is unable to compete in the new global economy.

It will not satisfy the public's interest; in fact, polls over the last few years show that the overwhelming majority of Americans favor national standards in education, to the extent even of wanting a national curriculum.

In short, if Congress removes the federal partner from the federal/state/local partnership that Democrats and Republicans together crafted to reconcile the urgent need for education standards with the American tradition of education governance, it will not be simply enacting a change; it will be resisting change and legislating mediocrity.

Why We Need Academic Standards

The subject of what students should know and be able to do is about as basic to education policy and practice as one can get. Every one of the advanced industrial democracies with which we compete has grade-by-grade national or regional curriculum frameworks, and in so doing makes clear its expectations for students, school staff, textbooks and other instructional material, and the professional preparation of prospective teachers. We do not. Every one of these nations also administers student tests that are based on its content standards, that complement curriculum and instruction and that students can study for and have strong incentives to do so; their class and test performance during their school careers will determine whether they go to college and whether they get a good job at good wages. We do none of these things.

If American students performed at high levels, we would say that our way of doing things is right and what the rest of the industrialized democracies do does not work. But that is not the case. I won't belabor you with statistics you've heard before, so suffice it to say that on every international comparison our students are outperformed. (The exception to this is reading, where we are about average.) We are not doing worse than we did before, at least not by any robust measure. For example, performance on the National Assessment of Educational Progress (NAEP), which has been administered for 25 years, is about the same as it was in 1970, with a dip and a recovery between then and now. And African-American and Hispanic student achievement has improved greatly over this period. But doing the same or even better by the criterion of 1970 means little because 1970 performance levels were low to begin with and the rest of the world has considerably outstripped our students.

Why is that? One explanation is our high incidence of childhood poverty, higher than any in the developed world. This explanation has been borne out by research: On our own tests and in international comparisons, poverty accounts for a great deal of the variation in scores. However, poverty does not explain why more advantaged American students do not, on average, attain high levels of performance – and why American students, who on the whole are still more advantaged than students in competitor nations, are nonetheless outperformed by students in those nations. And poverty does not explain why non-public schools, which select their students and have a relatively advantaged student body, have such a low percentage of students in the top levels of NAEP, or why, once you control for family background, public and non-public school achievement is at about the same mediocre level.

If you were in a business and not doing well, you'd look at what your successful competitors were doing for clues. None of our competitors (with the exception of England, which is in worse educational shape than we are in) has a school board in every school or other forms of radical decentralization or charter schools or private management of its public schools or any of the other untested reforms du jour we routinely embrace as panaceas. And none of them uses choice or competition as an instrument of school improvement. What they all have is clear and rigorous academic standards for students – in fact, curriculum frameworks – and education systems whose every part, from governance to funding, textbooks to tests, principals to teachers, operates within that academic framework.

This is plain common sense. No business or organization could successfully operate without knowing clearly what its product was supposed to be (or getting conflicting messages about it), what quality standards it must meet and how to measure whether or not it is meeting its goals. And yet, up until recently, this is how our education system has been asked to operate. It is a wonder we have done as well as we have. It is no wonder we have been doing so poorly.

Where Did the Standards Movement Come From?

There has lately been an effort to portray the standards movement in general and Goals 2000: Educate America Act in particular as creatures of the "education establishment" and the Democratic party. This is revisionist history. If you look at A Nation at Risk, brought out in 1983 under the Reagan administration, you'll see in it an unequivocal call for clear and rigorous academic standards. And if you remember, most of the education establishment did not exactly warm to the report.

Many things were done in the name of A Nation at Risk, but few of them followed up on the report's central message about standards. It took until 1989, when George Bush was President and Bill Clinton the governor of Arkansas and a leading member of the National Governors' Association (NGA), for the standards movement to begin. In that year, Bush gathered the nation's governors at an historic Education Summit in Charlottesville, Virginia, and united them in an unprecedented agreement to establish national education goals. There was also agreement that without a national strategy for reaching the goals, we would never achieve them.

The six national education goals were formally adopted in January 1990 by the NGA and President Bush, who launched an America 2000 initiative to encourage broad buy-in to the goals. A few months later, the President and governors created the National Education Goals Panel (NEGP) to bring further attention to the goals and to monitor progress toward meeting them. But as NEGP realized, that was easier said than done. Goal 3, for example, said: "By the year 2000, American students will leave grades 4, 8 and 12 having demonstrated competency over challenging subject matter, including English, mathematics, science, foreign languages, civics and government, economics, arts, history and geography, and every school in America will ensure that all students learn to use their minds well, so they may be prepared for responsible citizenship, further learning, and productive employment in our modern economy." But what were our standards for competency? What did challenging subject matter consist of? What was the relevant content in the vast fields of English, math, science, history...? How could we know whether we were making progress toward meeting that goal without addressing these questions? How would students and schools know what was expected of them?

As NEGP observed, "Creating a world-class education system means finding out what students actually know and can do. But determining this is not so simple. The kind of information needed goes beyond traditional methods of testing and reporting. We need to specify our expectations for student performance, making sure that they are high enough to match the highest levels in the world, and we need to determine how many students meet these expectations." NEGP then went on to recommend the establishment of such standards, "along with a voluntary national system of examinations (not a single national test) to tell us whether or not the standards are being met." (The National Education Goals Report: Building a Nation of Learners, National Education Goals Panel, Washington, D.C., 1991.)

In June 1991, Congress authorized a bipartisan National Council on Education Standards and Testing (NCEST, on which I served) to advise the public about whether national education standards should and can be established and whether, "while respecting state and local control of education, an appropriate system of voluntary national tests or examinations should and can be established." (P.L. 102-62) (Note: Secretary of Education Lamar Alexander went much farther than this by proposing federal tests, New American Achievement tests, that would be produced even before the issue of national standards had been settled.)

NCEST's report was released in January 1992, and it said yes to the two main questions posed by Congress. As co-chairs Governor Carroll Campbell (Republican, South Carolina) and Governor Roy Romer (Democrat, Colorado) stated in their introduction, "We believe this report is an important contribution in moving the Nation toward the adoption of high national education standards for all students and a voluntary, linked system of assessments.... Through its deliberations, the Council found that the absence of explicit national standards keyed to world-class levels of performance severely hampers our ability to monitor the Nation's progress toward the National Education Goals."

NCEST further stipulated that the standards be national and not federal and that buy-in ought to be at the discretion of the states rather than federally mandated; that the standards must reflect high expectations and provide focus and direction but not become a national curriculum; and that standards must be dynamic rather than fixed forever. NCEST further recommended a national system of assessments, composed of individual student assessments and large-scale sample assessments, such as NAEP. Such a national system, the report said, must consist of multiple methods of measuring progress and not a single test, and it must be voluntary. Eventually, however, NCEST continued, assessments "could be used for such high-stakes purposes as high school graduation, college admission, continuing education, and certification for employment" and by states and localities "as the basis for system accountability."

Although NCEST did not want the federal government to mandate or directly develop either standards or assessments, it concluded that some mechanism for coordination and quality control was necessary. It therefore recommended that the original NEGP be reconfigured to be more politically representative and that the new NEGP appoint a National Education Standards and Assessment Council to certify standards and the assessments based on them as world class. No one dissented from this recommendation about a federal role in certifying standards and the assessments based on them as world class (or on any other recommendation), no one including members of the Bush administration – Lynne Cheney, Chester Finn, David Kearns and Roger Porter – or Senators Jeff Bingaman and Orrin Hatch or Representatives William Goodling and Dale Kildee. Yet it is this bipartisan recommendation that is now threatening Goals 2000 and the progress of the standards movement.

Goals 2000: Educate America Act

Six years and a lot of hard, bipartisan work by Congress, the business community and educators went into Goals 2000, which in the main encourages states to develop challenging academic standards for students. Goals 2000 is an invitation, not a mandate, and 44 states have already accepted that invitation. Moreover, Goals 2000 was explicitly designed to give maximum flexibility to the states in developing their standards and reform plans. And it gives the same flexibility to local districts in determining how students will meet standards. In fact, Goals 2000 is the least prescriptive federal education law devised. Recent efforts to portray it as intruding a heavy federal hand into our tradition of state and local control of education are seriously misguided.

National Education Standards and Improvement Council

By all accounts, the sticking point on Goals 2000 is the National Education Standards and Improvement Council (NESIC). NESIC is supposed to work together with the National Education Goals Panel to establish criteria for certifying standards as internationally competitive and then review and certify standards that are voluntarily submitted to them. National standards may be voluntarily submitted by professional or other organizations, and states may also voluntarily submit their standards for review and certification based on international comparisons.

If NESIC threatens the progress of Goals 2000 and our incipient standards movement, then I say let's dispense with NESIC. But states and other entities have asked for and need the opportunity to have the academic standards they develop benchmarked to the best in the world, and they should not be expected to do that on their own. I would say that more strongly: They cannot do that on their own. As evidence, I would present the vague and largely non-academic standards many states have been producing. As evidence, I would cite the fact that this has happened despite the existence of a few decent state and other standards that states and localities beginning their standards effort did not consult. And as evidence, I would cite the fact that no state, not even the ones most advanced on the standards effort, has yet

92-107 O - 95 - 3

attempted to look at international standards; in fact, I think the AFT has done more work in this area than any state.

To be sure, some of these sets of state standards have come in for criticism from within their respective states, as well as support. But both the criticism and support seem to be no more than matters of opinion or ideology; there are precious few people in the nation, let alone within a state, that know what world-class standards look like and what students are really capable of doing. Until that knowledge is widespread, the quality of a state's or any other entity's standards will be no more than a matter of opinion. And that's just not good enough. It is essential to have some representative, knowledgeable and independent body to enable them and the public at large to assess objectively the quality and rigor of the standards. This is clearly, and urgently, in the national interest, and when the national interest is at issue, a federal role is fit and appropriate.

There is another, practical reason for reaffirming the basic purpose of a NESIC, albeit in a different form, and for carrying on the indirect federal role in national standards. As the original, bipartisan National Education Goals Panel and the bipartisan National Council on Education Standards and Testing recognized shortly after the national education goals were adopted, the national education goals are useless if there are no recognized national academic standards that meet internationally competitive criteria to enable us to measure progress toward achievement of the goals. Witness, for example, the cobbled if valiant way the current National Education Goals Panel has had to report on our progress toward meeting the goals. And without such recognized standards (and a body capable of recognizing them as world class), how will states and other entities know whether their own standards are competitive enough to enable their students to achieve the goals? And without such standards, how will teachers know what is expected of them, students know what is required of them and parents know how to judge their children's progress? How will the public ever get a comprehensible picture of how their tax dollars are supposed to be spent and with what educational results? And how will we ever have a sane accountability system for students and schools?

The question, or rather the fear, has been raised that any alternative to NESIC that nonetheless develops criteria for world-class standards and issues reviews of voluntarily submitted standards according to these criteria would bear the taint of a "national school board" if it involved any federal role, no matter how indirect. I understand the fear but urge that it be met with forceful leadership. Judging from the public's overwhelming support of national standards, to the extent of favoring a national curriculum, there is nothing to fear from the public.

In conclusion, let me say in the strongest possible terms, reaffirm your support for Goals 2000, the standards movement and the national education goals. Parents, teachers and the public are strongly behind this movement. Certainly business is. We have been searching long and hard for how the national interest in having students reach higher achievement levels can be pursued in a way that is both forward looking and respectful of the American tradition in education: local control, state responsibility and federal help. Goals 2000 is that vehicle. It is incumbent upon all of us to settle quickly any controversy and allow the standards movement to go forward.

Chairman HOEKSTRA. Thank you. Dr. Ravitch.

STATEMENT OF DR. DIANE RAVITCH, NEW YORK UNIVERSITY, NEW YORK, NEW YORK

Dr. RAVITCH. Thank you. I would like to introduce myself. In addition to being a Senior Scholar at New York University, I'm a Senior Fellow at Brookings Institution but, more importantly for this discussion, I was Assistant Secretary of Education during the last two years of the Bush Administration.

I'm delighted to be here before this committee, and particularly to see people on both sides of the aisle, who were extremely helpful to me, and I'm much more accustomed to being battered down than being welcomed, so it's a delight, indeed, to be here today.

I also should mention, Mr. Hoekstra—you referred to my book—I spent a year after leaving the Bush Administration, writing a book about national standards that explained why there was bipartisan effort to create national standards, what the good reasons were for having them and what some of the dangers are, in moving in that direction. I'm sorry that I didn't bring a copy of the book, but it exists.

Since so many of those who preceded me have stated some of the important reasons for having national standards as well as some of the cautions, I want to skip that part of the discussion and say that the bottom line is that we have, as Senator Bingaman had said, low national standards today, based on dumbed-down textbooks and, in many cases, mass market tests in which the kids learn to be very good guessers, but don't necessarily demonstrate that they've learned very much. And our low national standards coexist in a world with rather high international standards, and that's why we find ourselves here today, this, after more than a decade of trying to figure out what do you do about a nation at risk, what do you do when you see one international assessment after another coming out, in which American school children are, at best, in the middle in math and science, and very often at the very bottom.

When I was in office, we got an international assessment in math and science, in which we found that our 13-year-olds and our 17-year-olds scored at the very bottom in math and in science, compared to even some countries that we consider to be far below us in terms of economic and technological development.

So, we do have a problem, and this is why, when I was in the Bush Administration, the Department of Education made grants to groups of scholars and teachers to develop content standards—that is, what should children know and be able to do in science, history, geography, civics, foreign languages, English, and the arts. We did this in collaboration with Dr. Cheney, at the National Endowment for the Humanities, also with Dr. Anamelda Ridicci, at the National Endowment for the Arts, and with the National Science Foundation as well.

It was our intention at that time—and I've had to reconstruct my notes—again and again to point out there was never any intention that there would be a Federal agency that would create mandatory national standards.

This whole development of NESIC and, before that, NESAC, was denounced by Secretary Lamar Alexander at that time. He said, when he urged the President to veto what was then called S–2, he said, S–2 would create a national school board, and I urge you to veto it.

Well, S–2 fortunately died in the Senate, but he never had any intention or desire to see a Federal structure created that would make these standards mandatory because he knew that as sure as night follows day, that the Federal Government would be conditioning funding on whether everybody was doing exactly what was in these standards.

So, I asked myself, having been on the giving end of the money, as Dr. Cheney was, if I had to do it over again, what would I do differently? Well, one is, in the writing of the contract, I would have said to each and every one of these groups, brevity—brevity.

I've seen the Japanese national standards, and let me tell you, the entire Japanese national standard for every subject in the entire curriculum is shorter than any one of those documents that you have before you. They are shorter than the math standards, and that's for every subject for kindergarten through 12th grade. They are shorter than the math standards, and shorter than the history standards, and there are very few that even begin to approach the idea of brevity.

Secondly, I would say that there has to be some kind of a screen as to appropriateness for children. If you read those world history standards, the thing that will strike you is, this would be great if you were a graduate student, but can you imagine a fifth grader doing research on the Emperor of the Ming Dynasty, and comparing the Emperor of the Ming Dynasty to the Emperor Suleiman, and then deciding what kind of a leader each of them was? Well, there's not a teacher in America who could teach that at the fifth grade level, let alone expecting that of a fifth grader. So, appropriateness is important.

Thirdly, I think that before something gets a thumb's up, there should be some field testing. I don't think any of these have had any field testing and, if they have, then terrific, but it should be there.

Fourthly, I think they should be nonintrusive, nonintrusive in the sense that the focus has to be on results—are our kids learning as well as they should benchmark to international standards. But, again, to refer to the world history standards, these world history standards are so totally comparative that it's impossible to say, well, we're going to spend a semester studying Japan. We're going to spend a semester studying India. You can't do that. They simply do not permit it.

The standards are based on the idea that everything that anyone studies about the world has to be comparative. Well, that's what those particular people think is the way to teach world history, but a lot of people disagree with them, and they've created or proposed a national standard for world history that many, many people in the field simply don't support, and it's very intrusive.

Fifth, I would say that it would be critical that every one of these groups should have the participation of real world people. By that, I mean people who are not necessarily scholars or teachers, but who are knowledgeable and thoughtful. And I would give you the contrast of a successful project—and I know that Charles Quigley is in the audience, but I don't mention it because he is here—the civics standards are, indeed, a successful project.

The reason they are successful is because Mr. Quigley and his group at the Center for Civic Education had the wisdom to bring in not only teachers and scholars, but people who work in the civics arena, as lawyers, as legislators, as judges, as citizens who are active in different kinds of community organizations, and they had sensible people of different parties saying, this makes sense, this doesn't make sense, this is worth teaching, this is not worth teaching.

I fear that that was one of the things where the history standards went seriously off-base. They simply had no idea when they released them, that people wouldn't say, aren't these wonderful. And a lot of people said they are not wonderful, and they are quite astonished because they didn't have that real world input.

And, lastly, I would say—and this is the hardest of all, but if affects the history standards the most—you cannot have national standards unless everybody involved in the process is willing to withhold disputed interpretations and methodologies, and keep it for their own classrooms and not try to impose it on other people's children.

And it's hard, but I think you cannot have national standards if they are going to become a battleground for people of the left and the right.

I would like to point out that of these projects that were funded, rightly or wrongly, all but two of them have been successful. The two that have not been successful, you might say, is predictable. One, obviously, is history because of the heavy weather that it's run into, the heavy criticism. The other is the English standards.

The English standards had their funding withdrawn by the Department of Education last year. The Clinton Administration Department of Education said they are not making progress. Well, the truth of the matter is, they couldn't even agree on whether English itself should be taught as a language. I mean, we had this problem negotiating the contract that took almost until the last day to get them to say that under certain circumstances maybe they wouldn't focus on English because every other language is as good as English, and except, and except, and except.

Well, if you can't even agree that the English standards should be about English, you are really in bad shape. Maybe we just won't have English standards.

I do believe we can have history standards. I do believe that you can get historians and teachers and sensible people around a table and say, what should American students know about American history?

And you can start of saying, surely they should know we had a Civil War. Well, you may have different interpretations of why it happened, but we should certainly agree that kids should know about it and have some discussion about why it happened and what the consequences were. And if you start with that point, you can get a lot of other things that you would add to that. So, I do believe we can have those standards if we can meet those other requirements that I mentioned.

Let me give you a reason why I think Republicans should support the idea of review by the National Education Goals Panel. The National Education Goals Panel, as Senator Bingaman said very well this morning, has more governors and State legislators on it than anything else.

More importantly, there's a word he didn't mention—it's bipartisan, and that's critical, because I have news for you, there is no area in the education world where Republicans ever had their views represented. And when Dr. Cheney refers to the education establishment, she's referring to a whole galaxy of organizations that have many wonderful people in them, but very, very few of them are Republicans. In many cases, they are rather shocked to discover that people actually register as Republicans. They think Republicans are kind of amazing people that you encounter from time to time in Washington, but usually in very small numbers, until last November.

But I think that what is critical for the Republican majority to recognize is, if the National Education Goals Panel has no review function, if no one has a review function, you are leaving all of these printed volumes called National Standards to the field, which will embrace them.

As a matter of fact, I recently reviewed the Delaware social studies curriculum, which Dr. Forgione has overseen, and it begins with material from the national history standards. So, they are already permeating State curricula.

I was recently involved in helping with standards in New York City, and the New York City social studies standards take from the national history standards. So, even though no one has approved them, they haven't had any real national review of any kind, they have tremendous outreach.

Dr. Cheney referred to the national math standards, and said she thought they had some real problems in there. Well, guess what? They are already in use in more than 40 States.

So, all somebody has to do is to have a consensus process within the profession, put out a booklet and say, these are the national standards, and they will indeed be the national standards unless somewhere along the line there is an impartial, nonpartisan—at least bipartisan, but hopefully nonpartisan—review where you can review all of the comments that have come in from the field, compare these to international standards and say, this isn't good enough. Go back and do it again. And give a real thorough critique.

I would hope that you will revise Goals 2000. I would hope that you would drop NESIC. NESIC is, unfortunately, too close to being a national school board. Drop the Opportunity To Learn standards, that was a political ploy from the beginning. I would urge you to drop the State improvement panels—that gets into the area of telling States how to write their standards. I think each State should be left to its own devices as to how it wants to write standards. And get out of this business that Congress got into heavily last session, of telling States how to go about setting standards and, in effect, prohibit them from having tests.

There's a lot of language in Goals 2000 that says tests are bad. I endorse what Al Shanker was saying, about the importance of having both standards and tests, and having tests with consequences.

I would also endorse Mr. Castle's recommendation regarding the National Assessment of Educational Progress. I think there are many districts that would like to be able to use the assessments.

I know in New York City, which has over a million children—it's larger than many States in this country—the chancellor would like to be able to use NAEP to find out how New York is doing compared to other kids in the Nation but, as far as I know, there is still a ban on using NAEP below the State level, even though this is a district that's larger than most States.

I would also urge you to basically remove anything from Goals 2000 that represents Federal intrusion, Federal sanctions, Federal requirements, Federal mandates, but I would also urge you not to abandon the effort to develop voluntary national standards, and I would urge you to permit the Goals Panel to have a role in reviewing any standards that are proposed as national standards, and to, in effect, offer a "Good Housekeeping Seal of Approval."

You know, when a recipe gets the Seal of Approval, it doesn't mean that everybody else has to bake their cakes that way, it just means this is a good cake and, if your cakes fall flat, you might want to take a close look at this recipe. Thank you very much.

[The prepared statement of Dr. Ravitch follows:]

TESTIMONY OF DIANE RAVITCH, FORMER ASSISTANT SECRETARY OF EDUCATION, MARCH 22, 1995

Honorable Members of the Committee, I thank you for the opportunity to appear today. My name is Diane Ravitch. I am a Senior Research Scholar at New York University and a non-resident Senior Fellow at the Brookings Institution. I am also the author of National Standards in American Education: A Citizens' Guide, published last month by Brookings.

I was Assistant Secretary of Education in charge of the office of educational research when Lamar Alexander was Secretary of Education. My agency provided the funding for the setting of voluntary national education standards in science, history, civics, the arts, geography, foreign languages, and English, in cooperation with other federal agencies such as the National Endowment for the Humanities, the National Endowment for the Arts, and the National Science Foundation.

I would like to explain why we did this. Since the publication in 1983 of the landmark report, "A Nation at Risk," it had been obvious that most American students do not expend much effort in their studies and that, consequently, they are on the whole far behind their counterparts in other major nations, especially in subjects like mathematics and science.

To galvanize action, President Bush invited the nation's governors to meet with him in a national summit in Charlottesville in 1989. The participants at that summit agreed to set national education goals. There was a broad agreement that American education needed to focus on measurable results, especially on improving student achievement. Two of the national goals were specifically geared to raising student performance. Goal three said that by the year 2000, American students would be able to demonstrate competency in challenging subject matter; and goal four said that by the year 2000, American students would be first in the world in mathematics and science.

President Bush asked Lamar Alexander to come up with a plan to help the nation reach the goals, and Secretary Alexander prepared the America 2000 plan. America 2000 was not a federal program, but a crusade to get every neighborhood and every community and every town involved in a voluntary national effort, based on the national goals, to improve schools and communities and the lives of children.

Well, the first thing we discovered when we tried to measure progress was that educators did not agree on what Americans students were supposed to be learning. Then we discovered that educators could not agree on how students should be tested. No one seemed to know what "challenging subject matter" was, nor even how to test to see whether students could demonstrate competency.

Shortly after I came to work in the Department, the president of the National Academy of Sciences approached Secretary Alexander and said that the Academy was ready to work with scientists and science educators in order to develop standards for what American students should know and be able to do in the sciences. The Secretary thought that made sense. Voluntary national mathematics standards had already been created by the nation's math teachers and were being used in more than 40 states at that time.

We were impressed by the importance of having clear and measurable academic standards for content and performance. After all, if you don't have any broad agreement on what kids are supposed to learn, how do you know what to test? What do teachers learn in their education courses if no one agrees what students are supposed to learn? How do textbooks get written that contain the appropriate material if no one agrees what students are supposed to learn? How would it be possible to improve achievement unless there is broad agreement about what children should be taught?

It is also important to note, too, that there are currently international standards for what youngsters should learn in science and mathematics. Our youngsters encounter them whenever we participate in an international assessment. Usually we find that standards in places like Hungary, Japan, Germany, Taiwan and Korea are far higher than ours; those nations expect more and they teach more than we do, not only to the elite, but to almost all students.

After we made a grant to the National Academy of Sciences, other academic disciplines presented proposals to the Department and, after extensive review, received funding. Those who got the money were supposed to identify what all American students were supposed to know and be able to do in their field. No one was asked to write a national curriculum or a textbook; no one was asked to revolutionize their field; the understanding was that they would conduct an extensive consensus process, involving scholars, teachers, and members of the public, and lay out only what was most significant in their field of knowledge.

Let me make one thing crystal clear: Lamar Alexander never

proposed to create a federal agency to supervise this process. He believed that any national standards would be strictly voluntary and that they would rise or fall, win adoption or be rejected, based on their track record in improving student achievement.

As I look back on what happened, I have several observations:

First, it is important to recognize that all but two of these standard-setting projects has proceeded without controversy. The proposals for voluntary national standards in civics, geography, the arts, foreign languages, and the sciences have been noncontroversial. (The science standards are not yet finished, but they appear to be on track.) Two projects were not successful. Federal funding for English standards was withdrawn by the Department of Education last year because of lack of progress, and the proposed history standards ran into a firestorm of criticism because of what many regarded as an excess of political correctness, multiculturalism, and lack of balance.

Second, we should not be shocked that some of these projects did not succeed on their first attempt. I take this not as a sign that the idea of voluntary national standards was bad, but that the idea will take time and patience to work out. We must have a means of seeking improvement of those proposals that were not successful. If our Founding Fathers had given up after the Articles of Confederation failed, we would have become 13 separate nations, instead of one nation with one Constitution. It may be that we won't have national standards of any kind in a field like English, because there are so many disagreements within that field, even disagreements about whether it is right to teach the English

92-107 O - 95 - 4

language instead of some other language; but I continue to believe that historians, teachers, and concerned members of the public can reach agreement on the most important issues, trends, and events that American students should know about American history. I believe it can work only if those involved agree not to impose their own interpretations and political views on what all young Americans should know about history. This is a tall order, but I still believe it is possible.

Third, I believe that there must be some national organization authorized to review proposals for voluntary national standards. The review process can be performed only by a body that is strictly bipartisan, that is insulated from partisan politics, and that is not an arm of the federal government or the Department of Education. The only agency that meets this description--in my view--is the National Education Goals Panel. NEGP by law is bipartisan; its members are publicly accountable; most of its members are either governors or state legislators, who therefore have an institutional interest in preventing federal control of education. There must be a review process at the national level, in order to offer an informed judgment about the proposed standards. Otherwise, anyone can put forth a beautifully bound volume called "national standards" and circulate them widely to states and communities. It is necessary to have some official body with the authority to review and comment on proposals for national standards in order to have some minimal protection for the public. I think that the Goals Panel should be able to express a view that is comparable to a Good Housekeeping Seal of Approval; this seal doesn't mean that everyone has to bake their cake in the same way, but that the proposal has been carefully reviewed and is highly recommended for its quality, its rigor, and its value in improving achievement. States and school districts are eager to have such standards, to help them in their own efforts to set state and local academic standards.

Fourth, even if we had excellent voluntary national standards, we still do not have any test today that will let schools and districts know how their students are doing compared to these standards. Right now, the best test that we have is NAEP, the National Assessment of Educational Progress, but Congress prohibits schools and districts from using it. I know that many people fear that NAEP will somehow be compromised if it is used for anything other than a national barometer. I believe these fears are groundless. Any number of states, school districts, and schools would like to be able to use a test that is comparable to NAEP so that they will have a good measure of student performance. I can tell you, based on my experience as an advisor to Ramon Cortines, the chancellor of the New York City public schools, that he would be pleased to have a NAEP-like test that would give parents and teachers a good assessment of student performance. Many states and school districts have expressed interest in using a NAEP-like test. I urge Congress to consider removing the prohibitions that now prevent states and school districts from using the advanced testing methods perfected by NAEP with federal dollars.

Last, I would like to urge this Committee and the Congress

not to abandon the effort to establish national education standards. There have been mistakes and wrong turns; there may be some more. But we as a nation should continue to seek to identify what our youngsters need to know and be able to do in order to be well qualified for higher education and for a high-performance workplace. We should continue to demand schools that have high academic standards and high levels of effort from students. It will not be satisfactory to wipe the slate clean and try to restore the status quo of five years ago. The situation then weas not satisfactory; our students were performing far below their capacity and they still are. American students need to be challenged, as do American educators. We must recognize that the rest of the world is working hard to overcome our lead in every field of knowledge. Our leading economists have told us that the most important resource of the twenty-first century will be brainpower. Improving the quality and rigor of education is critical to our future, and we must not shrink from the challenge.

Thank you for the opportunity to appear today.

Chairman HOEKSTRA. Mr. Burge.

STATEMENT OF MR. JAMES BURGE, CORPORATE VICE PRESIDENT FOR GOVERNMENT RELATIONS, MOTOROLA, WASHINGTON, DC

Mr. BURGE. Thank you, Mr. Chairman. I am Jim Burge, Corporate Vice President with Motorola, and I'm also on the National Alliance of Business Council on Workforce Excellence. My comments are on behalf of NAB and Motorola.

Frankly, Mr. Chairman and Members of this committee, I am shocked by the testimony that we've heard in this last hour and a half. I'm shocked not because of what has been said, but because of what hasn't been said.

I think we all want our youth to be prepared to be socially responsible. I think we want our youth to be prepared to be good citizens. We also want our youth to be prepared for economic independence, and that, gentlemen on the committee, means ability to get a job.

I think there's a disconnect between the world of work and the world of education that we haven't talked about. In order to set the scene, I'd like to share with you one company's view of the changing world of work and the skills and the kinds of competencies that we need in today's workplace.

Motorola is a leading provider of wireless communications, semiconductors, advanced electronic systems. We have, over the last five years, increased our revenues by 131 percent. We now have sales of $22 billion per year. We have 132,000 associates around the world and, over the last five years, we've created 28,000 new high-skill, high-pay jobs.

Our fundamental objective is that of total customer satisfaction, delivering to our customers the best product and services in the world. And a constant that has been with us from the beginning is uncompromising integrity and respect for our people.

We've concluded that our competition can make the same kind of capital investments that we make. We've concluded that technology only gives us a momentary advantage in the marketplace. But the real, long-term, sustainable, competitive advantage in a global marketplace is our ability to invest in and effectively involving our associates at all levels in the corporation.

Last year, we spent over $135 million in the training and education of our workforce. We require that each one of our associates have at least 40 hours of training, and many of our businesses are investing twice that amount.

We've delegated decisionmaking to educated and empowered problem-solving teams. They schedule work. They track inventory. They deal with vendors. They help us make equipment purchases. They meet with customers. They manage our quality and productivity. And they have assumed some bit of ownership for the success of our business.

Now, think about the skills that are needed to perform these entry level tasks. At Motorola, we share information with everyone, and we allow our associates to make mistakes. We believe that to take no risk is the greatest risk of all.

Our associates at Motorola are building a culture, they are enhancing their own future job security, and they are helping Motorola compete in the global marketplace.

We believe that empowered associates can routinely accomplish the unexpected, when given the education and the authority to do so.

We have documented savings since 1987, of reduced manufacturing costs to the tune of $6.6 billion—that's a "b"—billion. At the same time, our sales per associate has increased by 169 percent—that's a productivity improvement of 13 percent a year.

Now, this level of performance illustrates the world of work and the challenge faced by students coming out of American schools. Knowledge and skills are the prime determinants of their future economic success.

Now, the Federal role must change. We can't mandate services locally, that should be left to the State and local experts. So, what is the appropriate Federal role? Some have suggested that the Federal Government get out of this role completely.

I think there's a middle role that we should consider. There should be a role of leadership. There should be a catalyst to establish some national skill goals. A catalyst for partnerships between business and the education community.

The Federal Government can play a role in spotlighting best practices. It can disseminate labor market information, and it can provide technical assistance.

Education quality continues to be a national concern. And the business community continues to have concerns about the quality of the new entrants to the workforce. The standards for future success in today's jobs already exist. They don't have to be invented. They exist in the workplace. They are the basis for hiring, for evaluation, and the promotion of our workforce. And those standards today are different than they were a few years ago, and they are still changing rapidly, as we adjust to compete in a global economy.

The most urgent issue that we should focus on is that these skills needed in the workplace are not visible in the school systems, students are unaware of them, the parents are unaware of them. And the tragedy is that it is the youth who will suffer.

The stark reality is that youth who cannot perform against basic workplace standards are not going to be employed in the high performance workplace.

Job applicants coming to Motorola must have good skills in math. They must have good skills in reading. They must have oral and written communications skills. They must understand problem-solving and teaming. And I regret to tell you that less than 10 percent of the applicants applying today meet these standards.

From the business perspective, there is a need for standards. It's a visible means, a tool for communicating information about what skills are needed in the private sector.

We don't need federally mandated standards. States and localities can set their own, based upon information that they get from business, from higher education, and from international sources.

They should be articulated in a useful way that can be used by educators, by students, by parents, and by applicants. And I would argue that standards for knowledge and skills should be integrated, one set of standards. They should reflect the real world of work, integrated into academic excellence.

This is an important issue for business, for the student, for parents, for educators, for without information about standards used in society and the workplace, youth are not going to be employable in the future. Thank you.

[The prepared statement of Mr. Burge follows:]

TESTIMONY OF
JAMES D. BURGE, MOTOROLA, INC.

BEFORE THE
SUBCOMMITTEE ON OVERSIGHT AND INVESTIGATIONS
COMMITTEE ON ECONOMIC AND EDUCATIONAL OPPORTUNITIES
U.S. HOUSE OF REPRESENTATIVES

ON "A BUSINESS PERSPECTIVE ON EDUCATION STANDARDS"

MARCH 22, 1995

Mr. Chairman, thank you for the opportunity to testify before the Subcommittee on standards for education and their relevance to our future economic competitiveness.

I am James D. Burge, Corporate Vice President and Director of Government Affairs for Motorola, Inc. I have public policy responsibility for a wide range of human resource issues. Motorola is a member of the National Alliance of Business which has held a longstanding interest in the issues of benchmarking educational competencies to world class levels. I am also on the Council on Workforce Excellence of the Alliance. My comments are on behalf of NAB and Motorola.

Motorola is one of the world's leading providers of wireless communications and electronic equipment, systems, components and services for worldwide markets.

With annual sales of $22 billion, Motorola employs 132,000 associates in facilities around the world. Motorola's fundamental objective (everyone's overriding responsibility) is TOTAL CUSTOMER SATISFACTION. We strive to provide our customers with the best products and service in the world.

The constant that has been with us from Motorola's beginning is the belief in uncompromising integrity and constant respect for people. We believe that our people are the competitive advantage. We invested over $135 million in 1994 to train and educate our associates worldwide. Every associate has a minimum of 40 hours of training per year -- many of our businesses invest twice that amount. The return on that investment continues to ensure the best deployment and utilization of our human resources to achieve superior service for our customers.

Our management structure and pay-for-performance systems <u>now</u> reflect this process of ownership of the business by all. Associates at all levels manage the business. Management provides the total work environment and leadership to make the strategy work. Some significant changes include:

- We have delegated decision-making authority to empowered problem solving teams and turned managers into leaders and coaches and our associates into business managers.

- Pay systems that reward performance have replaced the old time-in-grade systems. Base pay is measured by demonstrated skill and flexibility through periodic job certification.

- We must share information with everyone.

- We allow people to take risks and make mistakes. To take no risk is the greatest risk of all.

Credible, timely, and actionable information allows our associates to attack problems and improve performance. We hold briefing meetings regularly in which the successes, competitive position, customer concerns, challenges, and goals of our businesses are shared.

Meetings are held by factory production operators on the manufacturing floor to review orders, identify daily and weekly accomplishments, and check the pulse of the customer. Manufacturing Coaches (formerly supervisors) make themselves available across shifts to ensure that accurate, timely information is shared with all team members.

Our associates are taking the opportunity to build a culture as they build a business. Empowered associates can accomplish the unexpected if given the education, then the authority to do so.

We have succeeded, because our commitment to quality, cost, and service to the customers through an educated and empowered workforce has saved us more than $6.6 billion in manufacturing costs since 1987. At the same time, our sales per associate have increased 169 percent. That is an increase of productivity or more than 13 percent per year.

We have committed to a process of continuous improvement that includes measures such as 10X defect reduction every two years, customer satisfaction indices (defined by the customer) in each business, and 10X cycle time reduction in five years.

This level of performance in a world-class competitive company illustrates the world of work our students will face coming out of America's schools.

Business has been interested in the idea of benchmarking educational achievement in this country to world-class levels for over a decade. The concern of employers, large and small, about the declining levels of education competencies and technological skills continues to come from experience with entry-level employees. Schools are simply not producing enough young people who will be able to compete successfully for the jobs of the future.

Companies, large and small, are facing the reality of a new world economy in which change is constant and accelerating, reaching every sector of our economy. To gain a competitive advantage in this turbulent environment, firms of all sizes are streamlining their businesses and becoming more efficient, more customer-oriented, and more innovative in their production and business methods.

For workers in this emerging American economy, knowledge and skills are potent determinants of their economic success. Increasingly, jobs with a future and suitable pay require education and training that many current workers, employed and unemployed, do not have. Employers want employees who are technologically capable and can show competence in problem solving, team work, initiative, and communications skills. Clearly an employee's future economic security and wage gains will relate directly to the knowledge and skills possessed by the individual.

The federal role in education and training must change. With today's rapidly changing labor markets, the federal government cannot effectively mandate services locally. The government must forgo direct management or regulation of programs, and leave decisions about how certain services are to be provided, and to whom, in the hands of state and local experts. The federal role of the future should be one of leadership, providing incentives and some financial support for state and local solutions. It should establish basic goals and be the catalyst for partnerships among the key players. It should provide accurate and timely labor market information and best practices from around the country, and technical assistance.

The Congress has debated the idea of consolidating categorical program funds into single "block" grants to states, and, in the case of education improvement, the debate has gone as far as suggesting that the federal government get out of education altogether and turn every decision over to the states. I would suggest that there is an important middle ground that allows for an appropriate role for federal leadership and assistance. The states and localities have always had authority over education, and there is still something very wrong with the quality of our schools.

I would agree that the federal government should stay away from notions about dictating or controlling education decisions that are appropriately state and local concerns. However, I would argue that education quality continues to be a national issue, a national problem, with serious potential consequences for our economic future and social strength.

The business community has been supportive of bipartisan legislation to encourage education reform in the states beginning with President Bush's America 2000 proposal through President Clinton's Goals 2000 proposal. Our interest focused on two national goals. First, providing information to the states and local districts that they could use as benchmarks for what young people need to know for economic success and good citizenship when they leave school, and second, providing states with financial assistance to accelerate the education reform they already have underway or to help get serious education improvements started.

Now, two or three years after specific legislation has been proposed for how to achieve the national goals, I would argue the case differently than I have heard so far.

Standards or benchmarks for knowledge and skills already exist. They exist in the workplace and are the basis for decisions about hiring, evaluating performance, and promoting. These standards are very different than they use to be just a few years ago. These benckmarks are changing rapidly, all the time, throughout the competitive global economy. They are changing in the level and breadth of competencies required for high skilled, high paying jobs.

The most urgent issue is that these benchmarks are not visible to school systems, to parents, or to students. The competencies are not articulated systematically, updated, or made widely accessible to those who need them. Even existing standards in higher education are not widely understood or accessible, but they exist.

The real tragedy is that our youth are the ones who suffer and will continue to pay the price for our failing to articulate standards of knowledge and competencies. The young person, who gets a high school diploma, thinking with some pride perhaps that it represents a passport to the future, is finding that he or she is not qualified or eligible for employment against the standards used in the modern workplace. The stark reality is that youth who cannot perform against basic workplace standards are not going to be employed.

The job applicants coming to Motorola must be adults who have learned to learn. They must have good skills in math, reading, written and oral communication, problem solving, and teaming. At Motorola, we regret that less than 10 percent of today's applicants meet our skill and education needs.

Therefore, from the business perspective there is a need for standards or some means to develop information such as international benckmarks used by other industrialized countries. Such benchmarks or standards are simply a visible means, a tool, for communicating information about what skills are needed in the private sector. Information should be gathered from higher education, from business, and other places where they exist to help states in their work to improve education.

We don't need federally mandated standards. States can set their own standards based on information about what is a world-class level of competence and performance.

I would summarize the issue this way.

- We need to have standards. We need the information from business, higher education, and international sources. They need to be articulated in a way that is useful to educators, parents, students, and applicants. Standards are simply communication tools that articulate essential skills for success in society and the world economy.

- The standards must be formed by the experience of business. They must be formed by workplace demands.

- Benchmarks for knowledge and skills should be integrated, so that one set of standards can be used for educational achievement and the future workplace. I do not see separate standards for education competencies and separate standards for work. Standards should reflect the real world of the workplace integrated into academic excellence.

- This issue is important to business, students, parents, and educators because without information about standards used in society and the workplace, youth are not going to be employed, or employable, in the future.

Mr. Chairman, I would be happy to answer any questions you may have.

Chairman HOEKSTRA. I'd like to thank the panel for all of their testimony. The great thing of it is, you've all provided us with testimony, you all agree, and we now have the answer, and we can move forward and pass legislation by the end of the year, we'll be all set, and in the next three to five years we'll have some of the best schools in the world.

The very, very complicated issue that you've laid out in front of us—and we're dealing with perhaps—not perhaps—the most important resource that we have in this country today, which, as you talked about in your initial testimony, is our children, and preparing our children to work effectively in corporations like Motorola, so that they can have world class jobs and get world class compensation, and it is an extremely difficult process.

Just a couple of comments or questions that I would have. You all have alluded to the situation that over the last number of years we have dumbed-down in this country. We have dumbed-down the education process, whether it's through textbooks and these types of things.

The industry that I came from, we worked on standards, and I'd like your reaction to two comments. Number one, what drove us actually to the dumbing down? As we're getting into more of an international marketplace, where we recognize that standards around the world are going up and, at the same time, what forces here in the country were driving us to dumb-down standards? At the same time, why wasn't there a coalition of people pushing standards up, and pushing us up to compete on an international basis, to be more effective, and if those forces weren't around over the last 10 or 15 years, what confidence do I have, or would this panel have, that the standards that we develop—because, typically, I find standards to be minimums. Standards just drive you to a certain threshold, they don't get you to a point where you're competing on an international basis.

I mean, we need to be striving for excellence and high objectives, and my experience has been that, typically, standards are just kind of a threshold. They maybe get you into the game, but they don't drive you to being number one. I mean, where did we lose this drive for excellence, and actually go in the reverse way, and who actually, in the coming years, is going to be this force driving this excellence? Any comments?

Dr. RAVITCH. I'm sure that every member of the panel has a comment on this. I think the driving force for excellence and for high standards has been a combination of the business community and elected officials because especially the governors recognize that in order to attract high-tech growth industries into their States, they had to have a well prepared and well educated workforce.

And you can look back, and there are books written about why standards have been driven down, but I think a part of it has been that there has been, within the education profession, a strong feeling that what matters most is the kids have to have self-esteem, and that if you grade them or judge them harshly or tell them that their work isn't good enough, or say the fact that you didn't show up half the year is no reason to flunk you, you're going to be promoted, so we get into this practice of social promotion, giving out good stars and enthusiastic comments on very poor work, and not giving kids the feedback that hard work is important and that you will not get good feedback unless you do hard work.

We have really deemphasized the importance of effort and education. There's just a ton of research that shows that to be true.

Chairman HOEKSTRA. How do we actually get at that problem with standards, or don't we?

Dr. RAVITCH. Well, I think that Al Shanker described it well, and that is, with standards, you say this is what you need to succeed, and then you have to have an assessment system that says are you meeting that standard, and then there have to be some consequences so that students understand if you are not meeting the standard, it's going to prevent you from getting into college, and it's also going to prevent you from—if employers say I want to see your transcript and see how you did on the test, then kids get the feedback it counts.

The problem we have right now is, students in this country can leave high school and get into college without a high school diploma. About a third of all postsecondary institutions accept college students who have not graduated high school. And a student can get a Federal student loan without having either a high school diploma or a GED. Now, what message does that send to young people?

And at the time that this Congress, or another Congress, was debating the 1991 Civil Rights Act, the Department of Education warned, if you pass the Act the way it's written, an employer will not be able to ask an applicant for a job whether they graduated high school. That will be a violation of the applicant's civil rights, and that argument was simply turned aside.

So, now you have actually written into Federal law that employers cannot say did you graduate high school. So, we have created a system that goes beyond the educational system to say that standards don't matter, that effort doesn't matter, that working hard in school is for chumps.

Chairman HOEKSTRA. Mr. Shanker?

Mr. SHANKER. Yes. Well, I strongly agree with that statement. I just want to say that we went wrong after—before World War II, all industrial countries only graduated a small percentage of their youngsters from high school. We had a different world. A lot of kids went to work in factories, and there were plenty of jobs for them.

At the end of the war, every industrial country decided that it wanted all of its youngsters at least to graduate high school, and a large percentage of them to go to college.

Most countries sort of sent out the word saying, do a better job educating more students to the standards that we have. In the United States, we had a different message. I started teaching in the early 1950s, and the message I got was, we don't want kids to drop out. They used to drop out. Therefore, lower the standards and give them passing marks in order to encourage them to stay in. And the kids in other countries met the standards that were there for them, and our kids moved downward.

Now, the other thing was that, basically, youngsters learn only by working hard. They've got to listen in class. They've got to do homework. They've got to seek out answers to things they don't understand, if they didn't get it the first time. They've got to work at it. And it's hard work.

Why do they do it? Well, they do it for the same reason that most adults work. Most adults work because they want things. And youngsters basically want two things: They either want to go to work right after school, or they want to get into college. And 95 percent of our colleges and universities accept all students, literate or illiterate, whether they've graduated high school or haven't graduated high school.

When I was a youngster, my parents constantly told me, unless you work harder and do better, you won't go to college, and they were telling me the truth. I worked very hard. Well, I turned around and said the same thing to my youngsters in the 1970s, they laughed and laughed and said, dad, no one works, and everyone is going to college. Of course, if you want to go to Harvard, you have to work, but I don't want to go to Harvard.

So, the kids know. They know that employers don't ask for grades. Employers don't ask for transcripts. Standards are important. Assessments are important. But unless we do something with those standards and assessments, then they won't count.

Essentially, colleges and universities, Federal loans and grants, we have power there. They say, look, you have a right to a college education. We'll help you pay for it, if you're capable of getting a college education, but if you're illiterate you don't go to college. We may pay for you to go into a literacy program, but you're not going to go into a university if you can't get such an education.

Think what would happen if McDonald's and Pizza Hut, and these other outfits that hire a lot of high school kids after school, if they said, we're only going to employ those kids who are doing well in school. Bring a note from your teacher. Bring your report card.

Think of how hard lots of kids—they would see that there's a relationship between what an employer wants and the work that they do in school, whereas now they get the opposite picture. They are never asked, what are your grades? They are never asked, is it okay for you to work this number of hours?

It's standards, but they've got to be connected to consequences.

Chairman HOEKSTRA. I'd just like to yield to my colleague from California.

Mr. CUNNINGHAM. Thank you, Mr. Chairman. I've got to go to a national security hearing, but I want to tell the panel, I've been here for four years, and this is one of the best panels that I have ever sat through. And, Mr. Burge, what you are talking about, I think the other members are saying the same thing you are, they just may not have said it, but I want you to know that—and I've talked to some of the other Members too, and they feel the same way—I personally want to thank you very, very much for helping us in this process.

Chairman HOEKSTRA. Dr. Forgione.

Dr. FORGIONE. If I could comment, I'd like to ask us to take a different perspective on standards. I agree with everything that we've been saying, but standards are more than a document. You can buy documents. But America can't buy this reform. You've got to build it classroom-by-classroom.

To have a standard means I've got a teacher who can teach to that level, and have a student produce the work that matches the quality product, and that's what we haven't had. It's not just dumbed-down textbooks, it's also low expectations.

We have to build into our standards examples. In Delaware, we built something called "building a backpack." Every kid wears a backpack to school. We gave him a little piece of material and said, how would you know—fourth graders—if this material could make a backpack?

It means you've got to design and experiment and control for one variable. I didn't learn that in high school, but kids can do it. As Diane said, we've proved special education children could do it. They needed more time, but they could organize their data. They could profile it. They could run the experiment.

We haven't had the good exemplars to show teachers what good teaching looks like, and what the products look like. So, I want you to think differently about standards being a document. It's only there if we have the work and the teachers to deliver it.

That's why it's so expensive. And that's why, as Lynn said, you've got to do it in public. You've got to bring teachers with you because, if they're not with you, they won't be able to do it.

Chairman HOEKSTRA. Ms. Cheney, I know you want to respond to this.

Ms. CHENEY. I think—you know, you could argue many analyses, set them against each other for what's happened, but I think that the self-esteem movement, the idea that kids ought to feel good, hit us at an incredibly vulnerable time when we didn't have standards in place.

And so more and more there was this emphasis on kids ought to feel good. There was no backstop there. Parents and policymakers and teachers had nothing to turn to to say, well, yeah, they are feeling good but, look, they've dropped down and down and down. So, that's the relationship.

The standards are sort of the backstop so that when things like the self-esteem movement come along, you aren't vulnerable in this way.

Let me recommend a book to the committee, by Harold Stevenson at the University of Michigan, called Learning Gap. And what he does is compare schools in Japan, China, and the United States. He goes to a little town in Minnesota, a little town in Japan, and a little town in China. And he does this at exactly the perfect age: First through fifth grade.

Now, after you get through fifth grade, then the Japanese and the Chinese start tracking their students in a way that we don't, so it's very hard to make cross-cultural assessments. But up to fifth grade, you can pretty much do it, and that's exactly when Harold Stevenson does it.

What he discovered—and I haven't read the book for a long time, so if I get it a little bit wrong I hope you'll forgive me—is that the students pretty much started out the same when they were in kindergarten and first grade. I think the Chinese kids were actually a little bit ahead, but pretty much the same.

But by the time he got to fifth grade, there were these incredible differences. The Chinese kids and the Japanese kids were miles ahead of the American kids, though they had all pretty much started out the same.

And what Stevenson did was try to figure out why this happened. And I'm not sure why he just looked at mothers instead of mothers and fathers, but he looked at mothers, and what he discovered is that mothers in the United States were much more easily satisfied with what their kids were doing, than Chinese and Japanese mothers were. They had lower expectations, or maybe no expectations. They were just very easily satisfied.

He told a story about a Chinese mother, whose little girl went off to school, and she came back with a 97 on an exam. And the Chinese mother said, is that the best you can do? So the little girl went back and she worked harder, and she came home with a 99. And the mother said, that's the best you can do? So she went back to school and she worked harder than she had ever worked in her whole life, and she brought a 100 home. And the Chinese mother said, yes, but how long can you keep it up?

You know, these mothers had very high expectation, and that's what standards help us to have. They help us to know when our expectations are realistic, or when they are falling, or when they are slipping. But none of this—putting standards in place so that parents and policymakers and teachers and students know what to expect—none of this requires a governmental certifying body for standards.

And I just would point out to you the fine work the States are doing. I criticized the math standards for not having long division or for saying that long division was going to get decreased attention. Not so in the standards the State of Virginia has developed. Not so in the standards the State of Delaware has developed. They are doing a very find job down here at the State level.

Just one last thing. I don't have the piece of paper for the math standards, so I'm probably going to tell you this a little bit wrong too, and I'm sure I'll hear about it. But in the math standards, there's this one package that says something to the effect of, well, if the kid has tried to learn how to add and subtract and he is not successful, don't keep pushing on him. Don't keep trying to force him to learn to do these things that, you know, he's just probably not going to get.

I've got to tell you, in Japan and in China, that would not be the mindset. We would have higher expectations. We would have the kind of expectations the State of Virginia and the State of Delaware are going to have.

Chairman HOEKSTRA. Thank you. Mr. Sawyer.

Mr. SAWYER. Mr. Chairman, my colleague, Mr. Roemer, has a meeting to attend, and so I would yield to him at this time.

Mr. ROEMER. I would thank the Ranking Member, Mr. Sawyer, for being so gracious. And I, too, would like to join in complimenting the panel. Oftentimes, I think people are tempted to come up here and be inflammatory and try to get a sound byte for the evening news, and I think all five of you have come up here with very good, helpful, informed suggestions as to what kinds of steps we can take to try to improve the process and work out the problems that are existing in this process.

I wanted to come back, Dr. Cheney, to something that you mentioned, and then you alluded to in your answer, dealing with Dr. Forgione's comments. You mentioned a State which was contemplating in-and-out types of problem-solving in math, that long division was out, that pencil computation was cut. What State was that?

Ms. CHENEY. It's not a State, these are the national math standards. These are what I've been calling the French model, the Japanese model, the models developed—this is trickle-down reform, if you will. This is reform from on high. These are the national math standards, which I'm not—you know, I've got a Ph.D. in literature, so I'm just kind of looking at these from a common sense point of view, but when I look at these from a common sense point of view, and I look at what the State of Virginia is doing from a common sense point of view, it looks to me like the State of Virginia has got its act more together than the national math standards do.

And let me tell you, I'm so brave to be telling you this because the national math standards have been widely praised.

Mr. ROEMER. Who put the national math standards together?

Ms. CHENEY. Oh, Al, help me—the National Council of Teachers of Mathematics.

Mr. SHANKER. At the local level.

Dr. RAVITCH. Math teachers.

Mr. ROEMER. Local people put them together at the national level.

Dr. RAVITCH. This was not something with any Federal funding, this was the National Council of Teachers of Mathematics. It's thousands of math teachers and math professors who, over a period of about eight or 10 years, developed these and promulgated them and said, these are what we consider to the best national math standards.

Mr. ROEMER. Thank you. Dr. Cheney, let me come back to you for a second, and then go to some other people on the panel as well, too.

What you've stated—I tend to agree with many of the things that you've stated, that we may have a problem with what some of these national standards say and how they've been promulgated, yet it doesn't seem like Virginia or Delaware are making some of the mistakes that the national board has issued. So, that doesn't seen to be as big a problem as it might be.

Dr. Forgione also stated that when he was able to give input on liquid science, they listened to him. It seems like we have some anecdotes where there have been some problems, but you seem to agree that the process of trying to establish through some give-and-take of some set areas such as math and science might be a good idea, isn't that correct?

Ms. CHENEY. Well, I'm really arguing that you don't want top-down reform. You don't want the National Education Goals Panel or NESIC or the Congress or the President or the Department of Education promulgating standards in any way. States are doing a fine job on their own.

And what the National Education Goals Panel might do is provide a coordinating something.

Mr. ROEMER. So you're saying that the Goals Panel would coordinate and give mutual advice, but not mandates, and that they would serve and give advice at the national level so as to recommend to Delaware or Virginia, you may not want to go with these types of standards, but Colorado or Indiana is doing something particularly innovative, and you might want to look at those types of ideas in math or science.

Ms. CHENEY. No, that even sounds heavy-handed to me. What I would prefer to do is bring together people——

Mr. ROEMER. How do you give advice? That seems like that's advice, to me.

Ms. CHENEY. What I'm thinking of as advice is, okay, we know that there have been standards developed in Virginia, and we know that there have been standards developed in Delaware, and you might take a look at those.

One thing maybe that would be useful to have the National Education Goals Panel do, as we move toward assessment, is come up with a form for the assessment, you know, that the students will take a one-hour test in history, and they might cover these areas. They will take a one-hour test in math—that's what happens in Germany. The exams in the various States have a common form, but what goes into that form, the contents that goes in, is solely the province of the State.

Mr. ROEMER. Finally, Dr. Shanker, let me ask you a question. You articulated many of the problems we have out there, the work ethic of children coming into school, the parental involvement, getting children to try harder in school. Where does this fall as a priority? You articulated some big problems that we have in schools. Is this going to be a panacea? I don't think so. Where does this fall in terms of trying to correct some of these big problems we face?

Mr. SHANKER. If you connect this to outcomes, it will come pretty close to being a panacea. It doesn't count. That's why the kids aren't working. But if every youngster and parent and teacher knew that whether or not you're going to get into a college or university is going to depend on being able to take an exam like one of these and pass it—or not one of them, but actually in four or five different subjects—I mean, take a look at what's done in every other industrial country in the world, for college admissions. If we were to do it tomorrow, we'd close up most of our colleges. You'd have to have some lead time on this thing. But you would once again arm parents.

I mean, right now, parents tell their youngsters to work hard, and the youngsters say, I don't have to, I'm passing, I'm getting good marks, I'm going to be able to get into college anyway. I mean, what can I do to get my kids to work harder, if the rest of the system isn't supporting me?

But if you've got a system that says you're not going to get into college, you're not going to get into a training program, you're not going to get that unless, then you're arming me as a parent to be able to put the appropriate amount of pressure on my youngster.

I just want to raise one point on the previous question. How do we know that these Virginia standards are any good? Who has looked at them? Who has compared them to anything else? How do we know the Delaware standards are any good?

It may very well be that if I look at those, I'll have the same sorts of objections that Lynn Cheney found with the math standards. Somebody has to look at these things and compare them, and lots of people do it, but you need somebody to coordinate that. You need someone with the technical capacity to be able to gather the kinds of material and information from States and from other countries, that no one State is likely to do.

I don't think our States currently are doing a good job. We're in the mess that we're in right now because that's where the decisions have been made. And if you leave the decisions there, you're going to get more of the same. Just remember that basically the States want to look good. They have low minimum competency exams. We've got an exam system where the majority of our kids are above average. That's how the tests are fixed. And if you put the solution right there—now, the States obviously have to play an important role in this, but unless they know that somebody's watching, and unless they know that they're going to be subject to public criticism, they're not going to do anything different than they've done in the past.

Ms. CHENEY. I just have to say, as much as I respect my good friend, Al Shanker, that this is old paradigm thinking. We are in a new paradigm now, and it's a paradigm that involves trusting the States.

And I hear so much old paradigm thinking going on on the Hill these days. I have great respect for my friends on the Democratic side, but we've been hearing it in the welfare debate—you can't trust the States. You can trust the States.

Chairman HOEKSTRA. We will get to the new paradigm now, when we go to Mr. McKeon for his question.

Mr. ROEMER. Mr. Chairman, thank you again for a good panel and a good hearing. And I'd like to thank the Ranking Member again, Mr. Sawyer, for being so gracious.

Chairman HOEKSTRA. Mr. McKeon.

Mr. MCKEON. Thank you, Mr. Chairman. I would like to know the definition of paradigm.

Ms. CHENEY. Well, it's a term that a lot of people have adopted. It came from a scientist named Thomas Kuen, who noticed that one day everybody would be doing science in the Copernican Way, and the next everybody would be doing science in the Newtonian Way, that the way of thinking would shift. It's kind of a fancy word.

Chairman MCKEON. I'm building a book of words that we use around here, that I'm going to try to come up with definitions. And I've got a few—one-stop shop, we're using in our committee quite a bit—and it's going to be interesting, I think, when I get this book finished, of all of these different words. By then, of course, we won't be using those, we'll be using something else. But last year, it was managed care, and a few other buzz words that we develop around here.

Essentially, I've been visiting with the Governor here, as I listened to you talk and comparing things. And I said, how do we come up with a standard? How do we get this? And then, how does this translate back to children.

He said, when he was governor, they sat around and they came up with some goals and it was three pages, and I said, do you still have that. Why don't we go back to that.

If we could come up with some simple list of rules that a person, when they graduate from high school, it would be nice, I think, and maybe we should go to Newt's correction day, and get rid of that rule where employers can't ask did you graduate from high school. But if we could come up with a simple set of rules or standards or criteria that when somebody graduates from high school in California or Florida or New York, and they go to one of those other States, that that diploma would mean something.

I guess it starts with that, and then we get people together and they spend eight or 10 years and they come up with this book, and then going with Mr. Shanker's criteria, who looks at it.

If we carry that to the extreme, if we don't like who is doing something in Virginia or Delaware, then we get somebody at the Federal level to look at it, and then if we don't like that, then maybe we should go to the United Nations, and if we don't like that, then we come up with some interplanetary conglomerate that looks at it. How far do we carry all of these things?

Ms. CHENEY. I think you need to think of all that stuff there as kind of commodities in the marketplace of ideas. And it's the States where the standards-setting should go on, where the primary effort should go on. As people sit down, they can look at all those ideas. They can look at the history standards. They can look at the math standards. They can say, well, this is good, this is bad.

I have, as a result of the debacle with the history standards, with foundation funding from the Reader's Digest Association, set up a committee to review national standards. It's entirely private. It's housed at AEI. And as the people in Virginia were working on their standards, they would call us and say, well, where could we find something like X. We'd say, well, go look here.

We just considered ourselves a resource. Maybe the National Education Goals Panel could do something like this, but it's already going on privately. If you want some information, call us and we'll tell you, you know, Diane Ravitch has developed a wonderful curriculum in California—framework for the study of history and the social sciences—and go look at that framework that Diane wrote, as you are developing your standards, and you will have everything, I think, you need to come up with a very fine document.

So, just think of that as material out there in the marketplace, and that's how we should continue to think of it. It should be a free marketplace. It shouldn't be a marketplace where you've got some government agency saying this is okay and this is not okay. Just let those things be out there in the marketplace, and let the States decide.

Dr. FORGIONE. Representative, I have a different way to answer. I'd like to go to one of your local high schools with you, and I'd like to walk down the corridor of the English Department and find three or four teachers teaching tenth grade English. And you and I both know, next to each other, different teachers who are demanding different things, and that's not fair.

And what a standard can do, if we can talk to each other—and these math standards are good now because we had six years to look at the NCTMs. It's not that the NCTM isn't any good anymore, we've gotten smarter. We've grown on it. It's a continuous progress model.

But even after you and I find two teachers who give an A and demand the same things, we're going to say, how do we know our child is going to be competitive in the 21st century, and that's why, as Mr. Shanker said, we need to have some way to externally review it. So, I do believe we need a review, but it's got to be efficient, it's got to be streamlined, it's got to be voluntary, because I want to answer that question for parents in Delaware, that an A means an A, and your A is as good as anyone's in this country, because we're going to have the best employees.

Ms. CHENEY. Can I just make one observation, because I'm from Wyoming. I don't live here. I'm like you guys, I live out somewhere else.

If the citizens of Wyoming went through what they're going through in Delaware developing standards, and they came up with standards that the citizens of Wyoming thought were great, and if you did have this National Education Goals Panel that could approve them, and we sent them there and the National Education Goals Panel said that's no good, the citizens of Wyoming would say, we don't care, these are our standards, we want them.

Dr. RAVITCH. Sir, I think that I have to differentiate a little bit with Dr. Cheney, and I admire so much about the work that she's done that I say this with all due respect. I think there has to be some kind of a review panel for this reason. We are dealing now not with a theory, but with a condition, and the condition is, she and I, serving in our governmental post, funded several projects. There is not a level playing field.

You have in front of you a bunch of books called national standards. Nobody has given them the title national standards, but they received Federal funding. Nobody else has gotten Federal funding, and I suspect nobody else will get Federal funding.

So, when one group has a couple of million dollars from the Department of Education and the National Endowment for the Humanities, and they go through a lengthy process and come up with something that they call national history standards, that has tremendous power simply because it exists.

And you will see—if your concern is that people be able to have other options—nobody else is going to get $2 million to develop national history standards. So, we have a reality of existing proposals, and if nobody says wait a minute, this is not good enough, this has to be redone, then they're going to have tremendous power in the marketplace because it's not a marketplace of free ideas with a level playing field. This is a marketplace where the deck is already stacked in favor of those who have already received Federal funds.

So, I think that there has to be—in my own view, the Goals Panel should play this function, not to certify, not to mandate, not to put any requirements on anybody, but to say, you know, I think there are some real problems here. We've looked at all the reviews from across the board, and we don't think these are ready to be called national standards. We think you should take them back and rework them, or somebody should come up with a better idea.

But absent that kind of a process, what has already been funded will, in effect, become the de facto national standards. If you like what's already been funded, and you like what's been produced, then one has to go with the position of no national review. But if you have concerns about it, as I know that Lynn does and I do and others do, then I think there has to be a process where there's a bipartisan but nonpolitical review.

Chairman HOEKSTRA. That may be an oxymoron. Yes, Mr. Burge, did you have a comment?

Mr. BURGE. Let me comment about the role of business in this whole debate. I think that businesses in the communities where I've been involved, are stepping up to this issue of ensuring that our local school districts and local communities are pursuing standards that are globally competitive.

We're doing a better job today of articulating what our needs are. We're doing a better job of partnering with the educational institutions. Unfortunately, there are too many communities where that is not taking place. So, the business community needs to step up to that issue in an ever increasing way.

One document I haven't seen you hold up and wave is the SCANS report, and perhaps we can replace that stack with something that's printed on one page, two sides. I served on the SCANS Commission, the Secretary's Commission on Achieving Necessary Skills.

During that period of time, we identified the competencies that were needed in a high performance workplace. In two weeks, I'll be sworn in as a member of the National Skills Standards Board. Title V of the education bill called for the creation of this board.

I think it's another opportunity for the business community to engage in a conversation with the education community, to ensure that the standards we are talking about are world class.

Mr. SAWYER. Mr. Chairman, why don't we inquire of our panel whether they are willing to remain, to allow us the opportunity to return, or whether we should try to do as much as we can in the next couple of minutes.

Chairman HOEKSTRA. I believe we have two votes, so the Members of the subcommittee will be gone for—it would probably take us 25 minutes, I would guess, if we vote and hurry back. We have three Members that would still like to ask questions. Mr. Castle.

Mr. CASTLE. I would like to ask questions, but not come back and ask questions. I won't be able to do so, sir.

Mr. HOEKSTRA. Okay. So, Mr. Sawyer and Mr. Green.

Mr. SAWYER. Let me just try to make a quick observation, and that is, we have talked a great deal about the ways in which we all agree, and the way that the panel agrees, and I take some comfort in that, but to be perfectly honest with you, I take greater comfort in the disagreements that we hear among us.

It is that which represents the fullest measure of the marketplace and the importance of the struggle that we're engaged in here.

Mr. Burge, we have been here before, and it has been the needs of the employers in this country that have driven change. I mean, at the end of the last century, we were in a position where this country and the world was changing as fast as it is right now. We industrialized in the fullest sense in that era, and we saw the explosion of the role of States and the responsibility they took in building education in this country.

We also saw another model when, in the interest of nation building, we set aside dollars from the expansion of the railroads west, to fund the land grant colleges, and it established a general set of goals that we expected of higher education that was different from what higher education had ever been in this country. And it provided a way for institutions of nation building, and the skills that we required in the American workplace, to proliferate across the country in a way that it never had before.

It was a Federal role. A national concern without federalizing higher education in this country. It hasn't to this day. It's a very difficult path to walk, and a fine line, but we can do it.

I'm not going to take up all my time, but let me conclude with this observation. It's one that comes from another commission, the Bradley Commission on the study of history, that I thought was a marvelous piece. Let me commend that to you, as well as an essay by Paul Ganion, in the November 1988 Atlantic, in which they suggest that among the goals that we need to have in the teaching of history—but I think it applies broadly—is to develop a sense of our shared humanity, to understand how we resemble one another and how we differ from one another, to question stereotypes, to discern the difference between fact and conjecture—we've heard some fact and we've heard some conjecture today—to grasp the complexity of cause, to distress the simple answer and the dismissive explanation, to respect particularity and to avoid false analogy.

We really live in a time when we've got to accept the burdens of living with tentative answers, where answers are not true for all time, tentative and sometimes dangerous and unfinished business, to accept cost and compromises.

I thank you all for being here today, and to be a part of that debate.

Chairman HOEKSTRA. Mr. Green.

Mr. GREEN. Mr. Chairman, I'll be as quick as I can. Let me say that I can see this is bipartisan because I disagree with Mr. Roemer on the panel not looking for sound bytes because—and I wish my colleague, Duke Cunningham, was here—but both Ms. Cheney and Duke Cunningham said that if it hadn't been for the changeover November 8, we would have had the history standards. But Dale Kildee was credited as helping lead that effort, and Dale is not a Republican. And, frankly, with 99–to–1 vote in the Senate, we've had two switches, but it's not 99–to–1 in the Senate yet.

So, I would say that maybe that sound byte might be a little more both from this side of the desk and over there.

Let me talk about the national effort—and, again, I always preface what I say because I spent 20 years in the legislature, and I know that that's where the issues are dealt with, and they should be, and in the local board—but in 1983, it wasn't the States that came up with A Nation At Risk, and it wasn't Washington that responded to it, it was the many States across the whole country that did that, and did a great many reforms, some of them politically unpopular.

We required a teacher test in Texas that defeated our governor. We required no pass-no play for football and, in Texas, maybe like Ohio, it was tough, but we did it, and now they're revisiting it 10 years later in the legislature, as we speak. But that wasn't because the States all or a sudden decided we're not competitive, that was because a national education agency, somebody, came up with that, and we tried to jump through those hoops to compete.

And that's why I was proud to be a sponsor of Goals 2000 because I, like Duke, have only been here two terms, and having that background and saying we need some type of national standards so the States will say let's measure up to it—I don't want them mandatory because no way that anybody in Texas would ever agree with Delaware on—because we want those same standards, but we also need to know that our math and our history—and I agree with Ms. Cheney about the history when I was looking at some of the things in there—we didn't want them to write the textbook, we just wanted them to write some standards, and it looks like they decided to write a textbook in these standards, and it's frustrating.

Mr. Burge, your testimony, back on page 7, I was impressed with it where all through it you said we don't need mandated Federal standards, and we don't, and I don't want Goals 2000 to mandate it, but we need to have some standards. So States can do it. And the business community, in the last 10 years since A Nation at Risk, have literally gotten involved in so many districts—you're right, not in every district—but we do need to have these world class standards that the States can measure up to, and I'll give one example.

A high school in my district that I grew up in, had a 10 percent college rate, going to college, 10 percent. A minority high school. It was a minority when I was there, and it's still a minority. They have a 60 percent attendance in college, going to college now, from inner-city schools, because it was adopted by Tenneco, and they provided both scholarships, mentorships through the school, and now they're going from the high schools down to the feeder schools in Houston, Texas, and working with them. In fact, Jim Kettleson, who is retired from Tenneco, still is active in it now in elementary schools. And business has done a great deal in 10 years because of A Nation at Risk, and I would hope we wouldn't throw out some of the benefits we've done.

Of course, I'm frustrated because it took the Federal Government 10 years to respond to the report that States have been doing since 1983, and here we are—and I asked some of the staff. I said, I wasn't here in 1989 or 1990 or 1991. I understood the fight over why we didn't see some Goals 2000 under President Bush was school choice, or a national test. Well, lord, we don't need a national test, and I don't want to decide school choice here, I'd much rather my local school board make that decision, or my local State legislature do it.

Let me ask a question of Ms. Cheney, and I share some of your concerns about the history standards, but I also understand that one of their efforts was to try to be inclusive, and I think we can have both. We can actually mention George Washington a lot more than maybe Madonna, but we can also reflect on that we are a Nation that's inclusive of everyone, and the successes of everyone as compared to Japan or Germany maybe, because we are that melting pot, or salad bowl as I've heard it referred to, and if you could comment on that, that maybe we could have the best of both worlds, we could do better on the history standards, but we could still look for inclusiveness to talk about the successes and the contributions through history.

Ms. CHENEY. Of course, and you're absolutely right, and that has never been my objection to the history standards. My objection to the history standards has been that they take this important principle that you and I agree on, the idea of inclusiveness, and exaggerate it to such an extent that they promote a new kind of exclusiveness in which you have George Washington mentioned only twice, you have Paul Revere mentioned not at all, and which all the scientists have disappeared from history. Perhaps, I mean it's hard to know exactly why, but many of them did happen to be white male, so this is a new kind of exclusiveness that's come along.

So, inclusiveness is something quite wonderful that we have accomplished in our textbooks now, and we should continue to hold fast to that principle.

Chairman HOEKSTRA. Mr. Green.

Mr. GREEN. Mr. Chairman, I know you and I both have to vote.

Chairman HOEKSTRA. We're going to have to run. I would strongly agree with my colleagues comments, especially Mr. Sawyer who said that if we would have taught the difference between fact and fiction, we'd have a much different debate about the school lunch program than what we've had over the last couple of weeks.

Thank you very much to the panel, it has been very helpful, and perhaps over the coming months we can again call on your expertise. Thank you.

The committee is adjourned.

[Whereupon, at 12:25 p.m., the subcommittee was adjourned.]

○